Editor
Sara Connolly

Managing Editor
Ina Massler Levin, M.A.

Illustrator
Sue Fullam

Cover Artist
Denise Bauer

Art Manager
Kevin Barnes

Art Director
CJae Froshay

Imaging
Rosa C. See

Publisher
Mary D. Smith, M.S. Ed.

THE WORLD ALMANAC FOR KIDS
Scavenger Hunts

Grades 6–8

Authors

Greg Camden, M.A., and Eric Migliaccio

Teacher Created Resources

Teacher Created Resources, Inc.
6421 Industry Way
Westminster, CA 92683
www.teachercreated.com
ISBN-1-4206-3853-X
©2005 Teacher Created Resources, Inc.
Made in U.S.A.

Table of Contents

Introduction

Simply put, *The World Almanac® for Kids* makes learning fun. For years now, this best-seller has fascinated children and impressed parents with its blend of eye-catching style and educational substance. Within its pages, science is explained simply, math is demystified, and history is nudged into perspective.

"The World Almanac for Kids" Scavenger Hunts provides activities that are stimulating, self-contained, and simple to use in the classroom. Students become detectives, using clues to search a piece of text for both contextual information and inferential ideas. Actual pages from *The World Almanac for Kids* serve as springboards for these lessons, which span the curricula and are designed to hone reading-comprehension and critical-thinking skills.

How to Use This Book

"The World Almanac for Kids" Scavenger Hunts is divided into five curriculum areas:

- **Science**
- **Social Studies**
- **Language Arts**
- **Math**
- **Across the Curriculum** featuring **Art, Geography, Health, Music,** and **Physical Education** lessons.

There are 4–6 lessons within each area, and each lesson is comprised of four pages:

Page 1 *The World Almanac for Kids* page

Each four-page lesson begins with a page taken directly from *The World Almanac for Kids 2005*. These pages present facts, statistics, and trivia in a variety of textual formats—charts, graphs, tables, paragraphs, bulleted lists, sidebars, etc. As a result, students become comfortable with reading and processing information presented in different ways. In addition, integral words and phrases are highlighted, circled, or boldfaced—thus teaching young readers to scan text for emphasized information.

Page 2 Content Hunt

In the Content Hunt, students become detectives who are given clues and asked to locate specific words or numbers in the text they have just read. The clues may be straightforward—for instance, on a page where "Japan and *Italy*" are mentioned, students may be asked to find "a European country." Or, students may need to think more creatively. In an article about the Earth's *crust*, students may be asked to locate a word for "a part of a pie." Also, if the text mentions "9 planets," students may be asked to solve simple math equations in order to find "3 x 3" or "the square root of 81."

Next, students are given sentences that are missing one or two words and asked to scavenge for those words on *The World Almanac for Kids* page. This activity reinforces their understanding of the material by giving context to the information. In a final section, students must use inference to locate items in the text.

How to Use This Book *(cont.)*

Page 3 Vocabulary Hunt

Each Vocabulary Hunt page begins with a word-association section that asks students to gather words that belong under a specific topic. Next, the students' knowledge of vocabulary terms is reinforced as they use clues to search for synonyms, antonyms, homonyms, compounds word, plurals, affixes, specific parts of speech, etc. (Students should have a prior degree of familiarity with these terms before using this book. The "Glossary of Terms" on page 5 can be used as a guide or refresher.) The Vocabulary Hunt page culminates with a "Take a Closer Look" component that examines and compares the structures and/or sounds of words to teach students about affixes, roots, definitions, and etymologies.

Page 4 Hodgepodge Hunt

The final page of each lesson presents a mixture of questioning formats. Students may be asked to answer multiple-choice questions, solve riddles and analogies, complete graphic organizers, and fill in various types of puzzles. An extension activity—entitled "Your World"— asks students to apply their newly-gained knowledge to some aspect of their lives. For instance, in a lesson about energy sources, students are asked to research their own country's reliance on imported fossil fuels and to consider the possible consequences.

These four pages may work best in conjunction with one another, but each is self-contained and can be used on its own as a beginning- or end-of-class activity. The lessons can be taught in any order; or, a curriculum-based section can be taught as a whole to reinforce a unit of study.

Additional Activities

The lessons in this book offer several opportunities for teachers to reinforce a particular writing or math concept from their daily lessons.

- Have each student write one complete sentence about the topic just completed. Specify whether the sentence needs to contain an adverb, a prepositional phrase, an appositive, etc.

- Have each student create a complete sentence that uses a particular vocabulary word from the lesson just completed.

- Have each student create a math problem in which the answer is an important statistic from the lesson just completed.

- Assign students—individually or in groups—to create their own Content Hunts, Vocabulary Hunts, or Hodgepodge Hunts. Have students base their lessons on a page from *The World Almanac for Kids* or on any article from a textbook or newspaper.

Glossary of Terms

The following terms appear in the scavenger hunts contained in this book. Your students will need to be familiar with these terms in order to understand clues and search out information. You may wish to allow students to keep a copy of this glossary to use as a handy reference for their work.

Term	Definition	Example(s)
acronym	a word formed from the first letters or syllables of a group of words	NASA, radar
adjectives	words that describe nouns or pronouns	green, honest
adverbs	words that describe verbs, adjectives, or other adverbs	actually, quickly, very
alliteration	when two or more words have the same beginning sound	the big baby blinked
anagram	word or phrase in which the letters, when rearranged, spell another word or phrase	Clint Eastwood = Old West Action
analogy	a comparison between things based on how they are alike	*cat* is to *meow* as *snake* is to *hiss*
antonyms	words that have opposite meanings	tall, short
article	word used to signal nouns	a, an, the
compound words	words made up of two smaller words	moonlight, backpack
conjunctions	words that join two phrases or clauses	and, or, but
homonyms	words that sound alike and are spelled alike but have different meanings	fall (season), fall (to drop down)
homophones	words that sound alike but are spelled differently and have different meanings	there, their, they're
noun	name of a person, place, or thing	mother, hospital, tree
palindromes	words or numbers that are spelled the same forwards or backwards	level, 2112
prefix	a word part added onto the beginning of a word that affects the meaning of the word	**un**kind, **photo**graph
prepositions	words that combine with nouns to form phrases	over the bridge, beside me, through the woods
pronouns	words that take the place of nouns	he, our, mine
proper noun	a word that refers to a particular person, place, or thing	Bob, Italy, Eiffel Tower
suffix	a word part added onto the ending of a word that affects the meaning of the word	art**ist**, photo**graph**
superlatives	word that shows the highest degree of something	smaller, friendliest
synonyms	words that have the same or similar meanings	little, small
verbs	words that show action	walk, thinking, went

Meeting Standards

Each lesson in *The World Almanac for Kids Scavenger Hunts* meets one or more of the following standards, which are used with permission from McREL (Copyright 2000 McREL, Mid-continent Research for Education and Learning. Telephone: 303-337-0990. Website: *www.mcrel.org*).

Standard	Page Numbers
The Arts	
Understand connections among the various art forms and other disciplines	89, 91
Understands dance in various cultures and historical periods	101, 103
Understands the relationship between music and history and culture	101, 103
Civics	
Understand ideas about civic life, politics, and government	33, 35, 37, 39, 45, 47
Understands the essential characteristics of limited and unlimited governments	33, 35, 45, 47
Understands the sources, purposes, and functions of law and the importance of the rule of law for the protection of individual rights and the common good	33, 35, 45, 47
Understands the concept of a constitution, the various purposes that constitutions serve, and the conditions that contribute to the establishment and maintenance of constitutional government	45, 47
Understands the major characteristics of systems of shared powers and of parliamentary systems	33, 35, 45, 47
Understands alternative forms of representation and how they serve the purposes of constitutional government	33, 35, 45, 47
Understands the central ideas of American constitutional government and how this form of government has shaped the character of American society	45, 47
Understands the importance of Americans sharing and supporting certain values, beliefs, and principles of American constitutional democracy	45, 47
Understands how the United States Constitution grants and distributes power and responsibilities to national and state government and how it seeks to prevent the abuse of power	45, 47
Understands issues concerning the relationship between state and local governments and the national government and issues pertaining to representation at all three levels of government	45, 47
Understands the role and importance of law in the American constitutional system and issues regarding the judicial protection of individual rights	43, 45, 47
Geography	
Understands the characteristics and uses of maps, globes, and other geographic tools and technologies	35, 39, 43, 63, 93–95, 103
Knows the location of places, geographic features, and patterns of the environment	25, 27, 37, 39, 41–43, 63, 103
Understands the concept of regions	37, 39, 41–43, 63, 103
Understands the nature, distribution, and migration of human populations on Earth's surface	37, 39, 41, 43
Understands the nature and complexity of Earth's cultural mosaics	37, 39, 41–43, 63
Understands the changes that occur in the meaning, use, distribution, and importance of resources	29–31
Health	
Understands essential concepts about nutrition and diet	105, 107
Knows how to maintain and promote personal health	105, 107

Meeting Standards *(cont.)*

Standard	Page Numbers
History	
Understands and knows how to analyze chronological relationships and patterns	21, 23, 37, 39, 41, 43, 45,55, 61, 63, 67, 89, 91, 101, 103
Understands the historical perspective	33, 35, 37, 39, 41, 43, 47, 53, 55, 61, 63, 67, 83, 89, 91, 101, 103
Understands the major characteristics of civilization and the development of civilizations in Mesopotamia, Egypt, and the Indus Valley	33, 35, 37, 39, 61, 63
Understands how major religious and large-scale empires arose in the Mediterranean Basin, China, and India from BCE 300 to CE 500	37, 39
Understands the causes and consequences of the development of Islamic civilization between the 7th and 10th centuries	37, 39, 61, 63
Understands the search for community, stability, and peace in an interdependent world	33, 35, 37, 39, 49, 51
Language Arts	
Uses the general skills and strategies of the writing process	11, 15, 19, 23, 35, 39, 47, 51, 59, 67, 75, 83, 103
Uses stylistic and rhetorical techniques in written compositions	15, 35, 39, 47, 51, 59, 75
Uses grammatical and mechanical conventions in written compositions	11, 15, 19, 23, 35, 39, 47, 59, 67, 75, 83, 103
Gathers and uses information for research purposes	8–107
Uses the general skills and strategies of the reading process	8–107
Uses reading skills and strategies to understand and interpret a variety of literary works	47, 55, 59
Uses reading skills and strategies to understand and interpret a variety of informational texts	8–107
Life Skills	
Effectively uses mental processes that are based on identifying similarities and differences (compares, contrasts, classifies)	8–107
Makes effective use of basic tools 63, 67, 71, 75, 79, 87, 93–95, 103	15, 27, 39, 43, 47, 51, 55,
Uses various information sources, including those of technical nature, to accomplish specific tasks	8–107
Mathematics	
Uses a variety of strategies in the problem-solving process	9, 17, 19, 21, 37, 41, 71, 74, 75, 77, 79, 81, 83, 85, 87
Understands and applies basic and advanced properties of the concepts of measurement	19, 69, 71, 73–75, 85, 87
Understands and applies basic and advanced properties of the concepts of geometry	85–87
Understands and applies basic and advanced concepts of statistics and data analysis	9, 19, 69–71, 73–75, 77, 79, 81–83, 85–87
Understands the general nature and uses of mathematics	73–75, 77, 79, 81–83, 85–87
Physical Education	
Uses a variety of basic and advanced movement forms	105, 107
Uses movement concepts and principles in the development of motor skills	99, 105, 107
Understands the benefits and costs associated with participation in physical activity	105, 107
Understands how to monitor and maintain a health-enhancing level of physical fitness	97, 99, 105, 107
Science	
Understands the composition and structure of the universe and the Earth's place in it	9–11, 13–15
Understands the principles of heredity and related concepts	9, 11, 43
Understands relationships among organisms and their physical environment	15, 17, 19, 21, 23, 97, 99, 105, 107
Understands biological evolution and the diversity of life	9–11, 21–23
Understands the structure and properties of matter	9–11, 13, 15, 25, 27, 97, 99
Understands the nature of scientific inquiry	9–11, 15, 17, 19, 25, 27, 83, 99

What Is DNA?

Every cell in every living thing (or organism) has DNA, a molecule that holds all the information about that organism. The structure of DNA was discovered in 1953 by the British scientist Francis Crick and the American scientist James Watson, building on research by others before them.

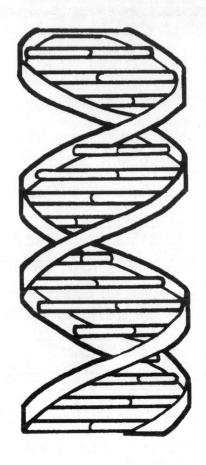

Lengths of connected DNA molecules, called genes, are like tiny pieces of a secret code. They determine what each organism is like in great detail. Almost all the DNA and genes come packaged in rod-like structures called chromosomes—humans have 46. There are 22 almost identical pairs, plus the X and Y chromosomes, which determine whether a human is male (one X chromosome and one Y chromosome) or female (two X chromosomes).

Genes are passed on from parents to children, and no two organisms (except clones or identical twins) have the same DNA. Many things—the color of our eyes or hair, whether we're tall or short, our chances of getting certain diseases—depend on our genes.

What Makes Us *Human*

The human genome is the DNA code for our species—it's what makes us human beings. In 2000, the U.S. Human Genome Project identified the 3.1 billion separate codes in human DNA. In 2003, researchers succeeded in mapping out all the human chromosomes.

The human genome contains 30,000 to 40,000 genes. That's not many more genes than a roundworm—which has about 20,000—and it's fewer than the 50,000-plus genes of a rice plant! But unlike most other genes, human genes can produce more than one kind of protein. Proteins perform most life functions and make up a large part of cellular structures.

By studying human genes, scientists can learn more about hereditary diseases and get a better idea of how humans evolved.

Find the following on page 8 and write your answers in the boxes.

1. a year	2. a letter by itself
3. an occupation	4. a number above 100,000
5. a part of the body	6. family members
7. 22 pairs + 2 =	8. something that wriggles

Use words from page 8 to finish the following sentences. Fill in the spaces.

9. Every human female has two _____ chromosomes.

10. All of the information about living things can be found in _____ that are called DNA.

11. Children have 46 _____, which they get from their _____.

Identify who or what is referred to in each of these remarks. (Note: there is only one speaker of all four questions.)

12. **I** am a British scientist.	13. **He** is my American partner.
14. **These** are the chromosomes that make us men.	15. Both of us have approximately **this many** genes.

Find three words on page 8 related to each thing connected to DNA. Write them in the boxes.

Genes	Chromosomes	Scientists	Cells

Find the following on page 8 and write your answers in the boxes:

1. another word for "a living thing"	2. a proper noun
3. a synonym for "couples"	4. an adjective meaning exactly alike
5. an abbreviation for a country	6. an adjective related to height
7. a hyphenated phrase meaning "long and slender"	8. a two-syllable word with a homonym of a synonym for "oceans" as one of the syllables

TAKE A CLOSER LOOK

DNA is an abbreviation for deoxyribonucleic (pronounced Dee-ahk-see-RY-bo-noo-CLAY-ik) acid. If you know the word parts, you know something about DNA just from its full name! "Deoxyribonucleic acid" is a complicated term, but there are many others that are more simple. Dihydrous oxide, for example, is H_2O—in other words, water: two ("di-") molecules of hydrogen ("hydrous") and one of oxygen ("oxide"). See what you can guess from what's given below.

Chemical Name	What You Can Guess	Chemical Abbreviation
carbon monoxide		
		CO_2

1. Which amount is closest to the number of genes you have? Fill in the correct circle.

   (a) one

   (b) one thousand

   (c) one million

2. Unscramble the letter in the anagram in the box to find the DNA code for our species. Write your answer on the line below.

MEAN MENU HOG

   _____

3. Rewrite the equation below, replacing the number *not* related to chromosomes with 0. Then work it out and write your answer in the box below.

   (46 - (22 x 2)) + 15 =

4. The shape below is called a **double-helix**, and this is what the DNA molecule looks like. Each part of it that looks like a rung on a ladder is made up of proteins. Think of three things about a person that are determined by genes and write them on the dotted lines in the double-helix.

   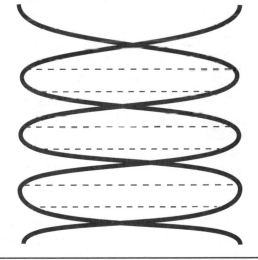

YOUR WORLD

In one sense, your DNA is who you are: it's the blueprint for the color of eyes and hair; for how tall you may be, for allergies and diseases you may have or get, etc. And unless you have an identical sibling, no one who has ever lived has the same DNA as you—so you are unique. However, you're even more unique than your DNA! Identical twins are often alike in many ways, but no two people are truly identical. There may be many reasons for this.

- Write a paragraph about what you think has made you who you are. Try to think about how your DNA has influenced who you are and about how other things and people have, too.

What's Out There?

What else is in the solar system besides planets?

GALAXY is the name of a group of billions of stars held together by gravity. Galaxies also contain interstellar gas and dust. The universe may have about 50 billion galaxies! The one we live in is called the Milky Way. The Sun and most stars we see are just a few of the more than 200 billion stars in the Milky Way.

NEBULA is the name historically given to any fuzzy patch in the sky, even galaxies and star clusters. Planetary nebulas come from the late stages of some stars, while star clusters and galaxies are star groupings. Emission nebulas, reflection nebulas, and dark dust clouds are regions of interstellar gas and dust that may be hundreds of light-years wide and are often birthplaces of stars. Emission nebulas give off a reddish glow, caused when their hydrogen gas is heated by newly formed, hot stars in the vicinity. Dust particles in some areas reflect hot blue starlight and appear as reflection nebulas. Dark dust clouds, though still mainly gas, contain enough dust to absorb starlight and appear as dark nebulas.

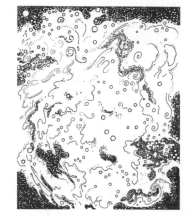

BLACK HOLE is the name given to a region in space with gravity so strong that nothing can get out—not even light. Black holes are most likely formed when giant stars at least 20 times as massive as our Sun burn up their fuel and collapse, creating very dense cores. Scientists also think bigger, "supermassive" black holes may form from the collapse of many stars in the centers of galaxies. Astronomers can't see black holes, since they do not give off light. They watch for signs, such as effects on the orbits of nearby stars, or X-ray bursts from matter being sucked into the black hole.

SATELLITES are objects that move in an orbit around a planet. Moons are natural satellites. Artificial satellites, launched into orbit by humans, are used as space stations and observatories. They are also used to take pictures of Earth's surface and to transmit communications signals.

ASTEROIDS (or minor planets) are solid chunks of rock or metal that range in size from small boulders to hundreds of miles across. Ceres, the largest, is about 600 miles in diameter. Thousands of asteroids orbit the Sun between Mars and Jupiter in what we call the Asteroid Belt.

COMETS are moving chunks of ice, dust, and rock that form huge gaseous heads as they move nearer to the Sun. One of the most well-known is Halley's Comet. It can be seen about every 76 years and will appear in the sky again in the year 2061.

METEOROIDS are small pieces of stone or metal traveling in space. Most meteoroids are fragments from comets or asteroids that broke off from crashes in space with other objects. A few are actually chunks that blew off the Moon or Mars after an asteroid hit. When a meteoroid enters the Earth's atmosphere, it usually burns up completely. This streak of light is called a meteor, or "shooting star." If a piece of a meteoroid survives its trip through our atmosphere and lands on Earth, it is called a meteorite.

Find the following on page 12 and write your answers in the boxes.

1. a color	2. a size
3. an amount	4. a length of time
5. a planet	6. "minor planets"
7. a half-century after 2011	8. a type of nebula

Use words from page 12 to finish the following sentences:

9. A "shooting star" is actually a _____ , and if it makes it to Earth without burning up in the atmosphere, it is called a _____ .

10. The moon is a natural _____ that _____ around the Earth.

11. Even light can't get out of a black hole because of the intense _____ .

Find the best answers to the riddles about "what's out there."

12. I don't hold up your pants.	13. Even astronomers can't see me, but I'm there.
14. I grow a head only as I approach the sun.	15. I can hold groups of stars together and keep light from leaving.

Find three words on page 12 related to each thing "out there." Write them in the boxes.

Nebulas	Comets	Black Holes	Galaxies

Find the following on page 12:

1. a word that rhymes with "colder"	2. a prefix meaning "very"
3. a homonym of a color	4. a synonym for "unreal"
5. a four-syllable word meaning "between stars"	6. a verb meaning "making"
7. an antonym for "expand"	8. an adverb for "totally"

TAKE A CLOSER LOOK

All of the names of the planets in our solar system have meaning. Most are named after Roman gods. Mercury, for example, is named after the speedy messenger of the gods because it is the planet that moves around the sun the fastest. Look at the planets below and what they're named after, then fill in why you think the names fit.

Planet	Named After	Why the Name Fits
Mars	god of war	
Venus	goddess of love	
Jupiter	king of the gods	

1. Complete this analogy:

   A ___star___ is to _____

   as _____ is to the

   ___Milky Way___ .

2. Unscramble the string of letters to find something both "natural" and "artificial": EELLSSTAI

   > **E E L L S S T A I**

   _____

3. Fill in the word chain of what's out there. Each word must either start or end with the same letter of the word before it.

G _ _ _ _ _ _ _
GAS
A _ _ _ _ _ _ _ _ _
C _ _ _ _ _ _
C _ _ _ _ _ _
STARS
S _ _ _ _ _

4. Like many galaxies, the Milky Way is what's known as a spiral galaxy. (See the shape below.) We live in one of its arms, and astronomers say that the Milky Way would look basically the same to us if we lived in one of the others. On each of the arms, write down a reason you think this might be.

YOUR WORLD

The world you live in is one of nine planets orbiting one star in a galaxy of 200 billion stars in a universe of 50 billion galaxies. Do you think there are other planets in the universe with intelligent life on them? Write a paragraph explaining why you feel the way you do.

What is Biodiversity?

The Earth is shared by millions of species of living things. The wide variety of life on Earth, as shown by the many species, is called "biodiversity" (bio means "life" and diversity means "variety"). Human beings of all colors, races, and nationalities make up just one species, *Homo sapiens.*

Species, Species Everywhere

Here is just a sampling of how diverse life on Earth is. The numbers are only estimates, and more species are being discovered all the time!

ARTHROPODS (1.1 million species)

insects: 750,000 species

moths & butterflies: 165,000 species

flies: about 122,000 species

cockroaches: about 4,000 species

crustaceans: 44,000 species

spiders: 35,000 species

FISH (24,500 species)

bony fish: 23,000 species

skates & rays: 450 species

sharks: 350 species

seahorses: 32 species

MAMMALS (9,000 species)

rodents: 1,700 species

bats: 1,000 species

monkeys: 242 species

cats: 38 species

apes: 21 species

pigs: 14 species

bears: 8 species

REPTILES (8,000 species)

lizards: 4,500 species

snakes: 2,900 species

tortoises & turtles: about 294 species

crocodiles & alligators: 23 species

BIRDS (9,000 species)

perching birds:

5,200-5,500 species

raptors (eagles, hawks, etc.): 307 species

penguins: 17 species

ostrich: 1 species

AMPHIBIANS (5,000 species)

frogs & toads: 4,500 species

newts & salamanders: 470 species

PLANTS (260,000 species)

flowering plants: 250,000 species

evergreens: 550 species

Fascinating Bio Facts

- One out of every three insects on the planet is a beetle.

- The Venus flytrap turns the table on bugs by eating them. This "carnivorous plant" lives in poor soils in the southeastern U.S. It gets nourishing meals by luring bugs in with its sweet smell. When the bug steps on one part of the leaf, the leaf snaps shut.

- The tiniest known seahorse, only 0.6 inches long, was discovered on a coral reef in the Pacific in 2003. The biggest species grows up to 12 inches.

- The orangutan is a kind of ape. In the Malay language *orang* means "person" and *hutan* means "forest." So orangutan means "person of the forest."

Find the following on page 16 and write your answers in the boxes:

1. a four-digit number	2. a word in quotation marks
3. a word repeated twice in a row	4. a length
5. a planet	6. a year
7. an ocean	8. (11 x 11) x 2 =

Use words from page 16 to finish the following sentences:

9. The word biodiversity means "variety of _____."

10. All people in the world are the species _____.

11. One-third of the insects on Earth are _____.

Identify the type of animal that is speaking:

12. I'm a type of reptile with my house on my back.	13. I'm a type of mammal who's more than just a big monkey.
14. I'm a type of fish who looks a little like I could be at the Kentucky Derby.	15. I'm a type of bird, and there's only one species of me.

Find three words on page 16 related to each listed part of the Earth's biodiversity.

Birds	Plants	Mammals	Arthropods

Find the following on page 16:

1. an antonym of "none"	2. a four-syllable word seven letters long
3. a compound word	4. a word in Malay meaning "person"
5. a word synonymous with "only"	6. a noun meaning "approximations"
7. a word that spelled backwards is some-thing you do with a knife	8. a geographical adjective

TAKE A CLOSER LOOK

You can tell a lot about living things by looking at their parts. For example, if something has no eyes, you know that it can't see—even if you've never seen the creature before! Words are the same. If you know a part of a word you've never seen, you know something about that word. You've probably seen the word "carnivorous" before and know that it means "flesh-eating" ("carn" = flesh; "vor" = eat). Look at the words below, and guess at what they mean based on what you already know. Then look up the definition and see how close you were.

Word	What You Think It Means	Definition
omnivorous		
incarnate		

1. Which section of the pie chart is closest to representing the percentage of bird species that are perching birds? Fill in the correct section.

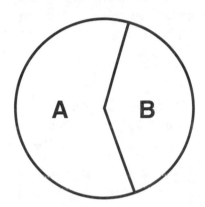

2. Decode the rebus below to find the name of a plant.

V + nus + =

_____

3. Which is not an arthropod?   Fill in the correct circle.

 (a)

 (b)

 (c)

(d) all are arthropods

4. Solve this riddle:

- I have wings, but I don't fly.

- I'm not a fish, but I'm a great swimmer

- There are more species of ape than there are of my kind.

What am I?

_____

YOUR WORLD

Earth is populated with all types of creatures—some of which seem to have similarities to humans, while others seem to have absolutely nothing in common with you and me. Choose two animals, one that you feel is *most human* and one that you feel is the *least human*.

- Write one paragraph that draws comparisons between the animals you've selected and human beings.

- Write one paragraph that shows the contrasts between the animals you've selected and human beings.

All About Animal Migration

The regular movement of animals during the year, usually following the seasons, is called **migration.** Animals travel at different times of the year to get the most from their surroundings. Their journeys range from tens of thousands of miles to only a few hundred yards!

Each year the **arctic tern** makes a 22,000-mile round-trip following the warmer weather from the northern Arctic polar region down to Antarctica. On the other hand, the **hummingbird** moves only a few hundred yards up or down a mountain. Arctic terns migrate over the sea—grabbing meals by diving into the water for fish. They stay in the Arctic only around 90 days before traveling south.

Other birds also log thousands of miles in search of warmth and food. The long-tailed **jaeger** flies 5,000 to 9,000 miles each way. Sandhill and whooping **cranes** fly as much as 2,500 miles each year, and barn **swallows**—which fly at speeds up to 46 mph—travel as far as 6,000 miles.

Swallows are among the first migrants each fall. Baby swallows and their parents learn each other's voices so they can stay together during migration. Most of the bird species that nest in the U.S. (520 out of 650 species) migrate south for the winter.

Monarch butterflies also travel long distances to stay warm, flying up to 3,000 miles to the same winter roosts—sometimes to the exact same trees! However, individual monarchs only make the round-trip once because their life span is only a few months. Their great-great-grandchildren return south the following fall.

Some migrations take place over longer periods of time. **Salmon** begin their lives in freshwater streams and rivers, migrate to the ocean as adults, then return to the streams to breed. They use their sense of smell to find the exact stream in which they were born. Fish that are born in freshwater, live in saltwater, then return to freshwater to spawn are called anadromous (eh-NAD-ro-muss) fish. Eels do the opposite and are called catadromous (ca-TA-dra-muss). They are born in saltwater, and grow up and live in freshwater.

Whales travel to cold water for feeding and to warm water to give birth. Humpback whales prefer the warm subtropical water off Hawaii to give birth to their young, so they make trips there each fall. Then they head north to spend the summer near Alaska, where the food is plentiful. They average only about 1 mile an hour—taking plenty of time to rest and socialize along the way.

Find the following on page 20 and write your answers in the boxes:

1. a double-digit number	2. a word in boldface type
3. a place starting with the letter "A"	4. 500 x 5 =
5. a speed	6. a hyphenated term with both numbers and letters
7. the children of great-grandchildren	8. what a person does after he/she chews food

Use words from page 20 to finish the following sentences:

9. Seasonal movement of _____ is called "migration."

10. Arctic terns go _____ after staying in the Arctic for _____.

11. Catadromous fish live in freshwater, but they are born and spawn in _____.

Identify the animal based on the statistical clues given:

12. flies as much as 9,000 miles in search of warmth or food	13. makes a 22,000-mile round-trip yearly
14. moves at an average speed of 1 mph on its migration	15. about 5/6 of all U.S. species of this type of animal migrate south for the winter

Find three words on page 20 related to each animal's migration.

Bird	Fish	Whale	Insect

Find the following on page 20:

1. a pronoun that rhymes with "gray"	2. a conjunction that means "in addition to"
3. a homonym of "turn"	4. a prefix meaning one or only
5. a lower-case abbreviation	6. an adverb meaning "approximately"
7. an adjective meaning "next" or "after"	8. a proper noun that ends with three vowels

TAKE A CLOSER LOOK

There are many different reasons why animals have the names they do. Some animals are named for certain features they have. For instance, a hummingbird is so named because it is a bird whose wings make a humming sound. Others, like the hippopotamus—whose name means "river horse" in Greek—get their names from other languages. Take a minute to think about the names of a few animals. First, choose one animal that you think is well named and give a reason why. Then, choose one animal that *you think* could be better named and supply your new name for that animal.

Well-Named Animal: _____	**Why:** _____
Poorly-Named Animal: _____	**New and Improved Name:** _____

1. Guess the animal based on these clues:

   • I'm not a fish, but I live in the ocean.

   • I eat in cold water but migrate to warm water to give birth.

   • I'm big and slow.

   • I socialize.

   I am a _____.

4. Complete this analogy:

   _____

   are to catadromous

   as salmon are to

   _____.

3. The birds below are listed in alphabetical order. On the lines to the right, rearrange them to show the order of shortest to longest distance of migration.

Alphabetical Order	Migration Distance (Shortest to Longest)
arctic tern	
crane	
hummingbird	
swallow	

2. Pretend the birds below are part of the thousands in a flock in the midst of migrating. Write on each one a possible reason why they migrate.

YOUR WORLD

What do you do when the seasons change and the weather outside gets really cold or really hot? Do you have trouble finding food during certain times of the year? Humans live in the same world as do animals that migrate—often even in the same places they migrate to and from. Why don't we migrate? Think about the differences between humans and the animals you've read about that do migrate. Write a paragraph on why you think humans don't migrate. (You can focus on either why we can't or why we don't need to.)

Clouds

Clouds come from moisture in the atmosphere that cools and forms into tiny water droplets or ice crystals. The science of clouds is called **nephology**. The names we still use for clouds come from a lecture given in December 1802 by the English meteorologist Luke Howard. Here are some of the cloud types that he named using Latin words. They fall into three main categories:

HIGH CLOUDS Cirrus clouds and other clouds that start with the prefix "cirro-" are generally found above 20,000 feet. (*Cirrus* in Latin means "lock of hair.")

Cirrus clouds are thin, wispy high-altitude clouds made of ice crystals. They often appear in nice weather.

Cirrocumulus clouds are small rounded white puffs that sometimes form in long rows. Sunlight can make them look like fish scales, which makes for a "mackerel sky."

Other clouds at this level are cirrostratus and contrails. Contrails (**con**densation **trails**) are man-made clouds formed when the hot humid jet exhaust hits very cold high altitude air.

MID-LEVEL CLOUDS Clouds that begin with the prefix "alto-" ("high") are usually found between 6,500 and 23,000 feet. They are high, though not the highest.

Altostratus clouds form a smooth gray or bluish sheet high up in the sky. The sun or moon can usually be seen faintly. (*Stratus* in Latin means "spread out.")

Altocumulus clouds are puffy gray blobs that appear in rows or waves. Part of the cloud is usually a little darker, distinguishing it from cirrocumulus.

LOW CLOUDS These clouds have no prefix and are generally found below 6,500 feet

Cumulus clouds are puffy whiter vertical clouds that get biggest during mid-afternoon. They form in many different shapes. (Cumulus means "heap" or "pile.")

Cumulonimbus clouds, also known as storm clouds, are darkish and ominous-looking. They can bring heavy storms, often with thunder and lightning. (Nimbus means "storm cloud.")

Nimbostratus clouds form a shapeless dark layer across the sky blocking out the sun and moon. They often bring a long period of snow or rain.

Find the following on page 24:

1. a month	2. a color
3. a Latin word	4. a person's name
5. an altitude	6. something on your head
7. a type of science	8. a word that is a shortening of a two-word phrase

Use words from page 24 to finish the following sentences:

9. Sunlight can make cirrocumulus clouds look like _____.

10. A meteorologist named _____ came up with the names we use to identify clouds.

11. Clouds are made up of tiny _____ droplets or _____ crystals.

Name the type of cloud described:

12. biggest during mid-afternoon	13. wispy; often appear in nice weather
14. name is Latin for "high" and "spread out"	15. shapeless and dark; completely block out sun

Clouds — Vocabulary Hunt

Find three words related to each aspect of clouds and the study of them.

Latin	Water	Contrails

Find the following:

1. a suffix meaning "the study of"	2. a hyphenated phrase meaning "created by humans"
3. an adjective in which a letter occurs twice in a row	4. a noun meaning an amount of time
5. an adverb meaning "usually"	6. a Latin compound word meaning "high heap"
7. a superlative meaning "largest"	8. an alliteration separated by a comma

TAKE A CLOSER LOOK

Cloud names are made up of different Latin words put together to describe the way the clouds look. Look at the cloud names in the chart below. Break the names apart—for example, altostratus = "high" (alto) + "spread out" (stratus)—then describe what the clouds would look like.

Cloud	What Are Its Parts?	What Would It Look Like
altocumulus	+	
nimbostratus	+	

1. Let's play Jeopardy!® (Remember, your answer must be in the form of a question.)

   Answer: It was from this weatherman's lecture that the names of clouds were taken.

   Question: _____

   _____

2. What word begins with "N," ends in "Y," and covers just about everything there is about clouds? Write your answer in the box.

3. In each one of the clouds below, write something that you have seen clouds do.

4. The diagram below is a word tree of different cloud-name parts. A word part can only connect to another word part if, together, they make the name of a cloud. Use your new-found knowledge of cloud names to complete the word tree.

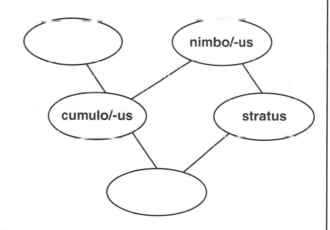

═══════════════ **YOUR WORLD** ═══════════════

Do you notice the clouds in the sky most of the time? What is the weather usually like where you live when there are clouds? Are there types of cloud-related weather that you've never seen?

• Make a list of all the types of weather events you've seen that are associated with clouds (for example, rain).

• Then, consult an outside source like *The World Almanac* or the Internet to find out what other types of cloud-associated weather there are, and list those.

Sources of Energy

FOSSIL FUELS

Fuels are called "fossil" because they were formed from ancient plants and animals. The three basic fossil fuels are coal, oil, and natural gas. Most of the energy we use today comes from these sources. Coal is mined, either at the surface or deep underground. Pumpjacks pump oil, or petroleum, from wells drilled in the ground. Natural gas also comes from wells. Natural gas is a clean-burning fuel, and it has been used more and more. Oil and coal bring a greater risk of air pollution.

All fossil fuels have one problem: they are gradually getting used up. There are special problems about oil, because industrial countries must often import lots of it and can become greatly dependent on other countries for their supply.

NUCLEAR ENERGY

Nuclear power is created by releasing energy stored in the nucleus of an atom. This process is nuclear fission, which is also called "splitting" an atom. Fission takes place in a reactor, which allows the nuclear reaction to be controlled. Nuclear power plants release almost no air pollution. Many countries today use nuclear energy.

Nuclear power does cause some safety concerns. In 1979 a nuclear accident at Three Mile Island in Pennsylvania led to the release of some radiation. A much worse accident at Chernobyl in Ukraine in 1986 led to the deaths of thousands of people.

WATER POWER

Water power is energy that comes from the force of falling or fast-flowing water. It was put to use early in human history. Water wheels, turned by rivers or streams, were common in the Middle Ages. They were used for tasks like grinding grain and sawing lumber.

Today water power comes from waterfalls or from specially built dams. As water flows from a higher to a lower level, it runs a turbine—a device that turns an electric generator. This is called hydroelectric power (hydro = water).

BIOMASS ENERGY

Burning wood and straw (materials known as biomass) is probably the oldest way of producing energy, but it still has value. Researchers are growing crops to use as fuel.

Biomass fuels can be burned, like coal, in a power plant. They can also be used to make ethanol, which is similar to gasoline. Most ethanol comes from corn, which can make it expensive. But researchers are experimenting with other crops, like "switchgrass" and alfalfa.

Recently, a biomass power plant was opened in Vermont. It turns wood chips, solid waste, and switchgrass into a substance similar to natural gas.

GEOTHERMAL ENERGY

Geothermal energy comes from the heat deep inside the Earth. About 30 miles below the surface is a layer called the mantle. This is the source of the gas and lava that erupts from volcanoes. Hot springs and geysers, with temperatures as high as 700 degrees, are also heated by the mantle. Because it's so hot, the mantle holds great promise as an energy source, especially in areas where the hot water is close to the surface. Iceland, which has many active volcanoes and hot springs, uses lots of geothermal energy. About 85% of homes there are heated this way.

WIND ENERGY

People have used the wind's energy for a long time. Windmills were popular in Europe during the Middle Ages. Later, windmills became common on U.S. farms. Today, huge high-tech windmills with propeller-like blades are grouped together in "wind farms." Dozens of wind turbines are spaced well apart (so they don't block each other's wind). Even on big wind farms, the windmills usually take up less than 1% of the ground space. The rest of the land can still be used for farming or for grazing animals.

Wind power is a rapidly growing technology that doesn't pollute or get used up like fossil fuels. By 2002, there was nearly four times the generating capacity in the U.S. as there had been in 1996. Unfortunately, the generators only work if the wind blows.

SOLAR POWER

Energy directly from sunlight is a promising new technology. Vast amounts of this energy fall upon the Earth every day—and it is not running out. Energy from the sun is expected to run for some 5 billion years. Solar energy is also friendly to the environment. One drawback is space. To get enough light,  the surfaces that gather solar energy need to be spread out a lot. Also, the energy can't be gathered when the sun isn't shining.

A solar cell is usually made of silicon, a semiconductor. That means it can change sunlight into electricity. The cost of solar cells has been dropping in recent years. Large plants using solar-cell systems have been built in several countries, including Japan, Saudi Arabia, the United States, and Germany.

Sources of Energy   Content Hunt

Find the following on page 28 and write your answers in the boxes.

1. the name of a planet	2. a percentage
3. one of the original 13 U.S. colonies	4. a temperature
5. 14 x 50 = _____	6. an occupation
7. a Middle Eastern country	8. a number that is a palindrome

Use words from page 28 to finish these sentences. Fill in the spaces.

9. Usually made of silicon, a solar cell changes _____ _____ into electricity.

10. A terrible _____ accident occurred in the city of _____ in Ukraine in 1986.

11. A biomass power plant in Vermont turns _____ chips, solid waste, and _____ into a usable energy source.

Name the energy source that best fits each of the following titles:

12. "Fission for Energy"	13. "Supplies Getting Used Up"
14. "Corn on the Job"	15. "Volcano Power"

Find two words related to each source of energy. Write them in the boxes.

Fossil Fuels	Nuclear	Water	Biomass

Geothermal	Wind	Solar

Find the following on page 28 and write your answers in the boxes.

1. a noun that rhymes with "wiser"	2. a verb meaning "to bring in from a foreign country"
3. a suffix meaning "the study of"	4. a homonym for a type of cloak
5. a compound word meaning "disadvantage"	6. a 3-syllable word made up of only 3 different letters
7. an adverb meaning "steadily occurring"	8. an antonym for "dormant"

TAKE A CLOSER LOOK

Look at the word geothermal. What are the meanings of its root words *geo* and *therm*. Can you think of another real word that you can "grow" from the root *geo*? How about *therm*? Fill in the chart below.

Root	Definition	Another Word Containing the Root	Definition
geo	Earth		
therm	heat		

1. What vegetable is ethanol derived from? Fill in the circle next to the correct answer.

   (a)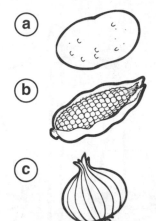

   (b)

   (c)

2. Which section of this pie chart—A or B—would represent the percentage of Icelandic homes heated by geothermal energy? Fill in the correct section.

   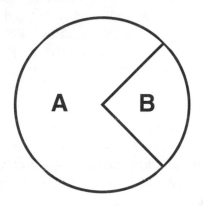

3. Fill in the energy word chain. Each word must begin with the last letter of the word before it and end with the first letter of the word after it. All words must be found on page 28.

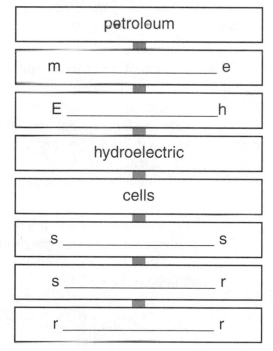

   petroleum

   m _____ e

   E _____ h

   hydroelectric

   cells

   s _____ s

   s _____ r

   r _____ r

4. On each blade of the windmill, write a reason why wind energy can be a useful source of energy. On the pole, write one shortcoming of wind power.

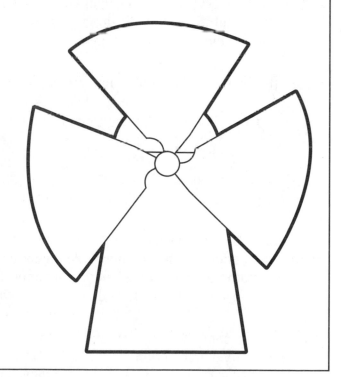

YOUR WORLD

- Do you know where the country you live in get its oil (petroleum)? Use the Internet or *The World Almanac* to research this information. Name two countries.

- On a separate piece of paper, write a paragraph about the affects that might result from a dependence on these countries for oil.

Governments Around the World

Among the world's 193 independent nations there are various kinds of governments. In most countries people choose their leaders; in some they don't.

WHAT IS A DEMOCRACY? The word *democracy* comes from the Greek words *demos* ("people") and *kratia* ("rule"). In a democracy, the *people* rule, rather than an all-powerful individual (dictatorship) or king (monarchy) or small group of people (oligarchy). Since there are too many people to agree on everyday decisions themselves, democracies nowadays are *representative* democracies; this means the people make decisions through the leaders they choose. In the U.S., these include the president and members of Congress. Mexico and some other countries also have a "presidential" system, where voters elect the head of the government. But many democracies use a "parliamentary system." In these countries—the United Kingdom, Canada, and Japan, for example—voters elect members of a parliament, or legislature, and then the members of parliament pick a cabinet to head the government. The leader of the cabinet is called the prime minister, or premier.

In a democracy people can complain about the government and vote it out of office, which they often do. Winston Churchill, one of Britain's greatest prime ministers, probably had this in mind when he said, "Democracy is the worst form of government except for all those others that have been tried."

WHAT IS A MONARCHY?  A country with a king or queen can be called a *monarchy*. Monarchies are almost always hereditary, meaning the throne is passed down in one family. In the United Kingdom and most other nations that still have kings or queens, royal figures have charitable and ceremonial duties but hold little real power—elected officials head the government. These countries are *constitutional* monarchies. But some countries still are *traditional* monarchies, governed by their royal families; Saudi Arabia is an example.

WHAT IS A TOTALITARIANISM? In totalitarian countries the rulers have strong power and the people have little freedom. Germany under Adolf Hitler and Iraq under Saddam Hussein had one all-powerful ruler or dictator. Dictators usually try to put down anyone opposing them. If they hold elections, they may be the only candidate allowed to campaign freely, or the only candidate on the ballot!

There are still some *Communist* nations today, such as Cuba, North Korea, and China (the world's biggest country in population). In these totalitarian countries, the government may run or control the economy. Usually the ruling Communist party is the only party that has power and only loyal Communists can be elected to office.

Governments Around the World — Content Hunt

Find the following on page 32:

1. a type of government	2. a country
3. a number	4. a hyphenated phrase
5. a set of initials	6. a Greek word
7. something you can sit on	8. a British prime minister

Use words from page 32 to finish the following sentences:

9. At the head of a _____ is a king or a _____.

10. Adolf Hitler was _____ of _____ .

11. China, which has a larger _____ than any other country in the world, has a _____ form of government.

Name the type of government that each country has.

12. the United States of America	13. Saudi Arabia
14. Cuba	15. the United Kingdom

Find three words or terms on page 32 related to each type of government.

Democracy	Monarchy	Totalitarian	Communist

Find the following on page 32:

1. a noun meaning "a group of people who are related"	2. a verb meaning "choose"
3. an adjective that rhymes with "dumb"	4. a proper noun with an "X" in it
5. a prefix meaning "one"	6. a compound word meaning "common" or "occurring often"
7. a homonym for the place in the kitchen where most people keep their dishes	8. a four-letter conjunction that has to do with time

TAKE A CLOSER LOOK

Most every type of government has a name that tells you exactly what it is. For example, a monarchy means "rule by/of one" ("mon" (one) + "arch" (rule)). Look at the make-believe types of government below, break them down into their parts, then write out what the government is like based on its name. (Hint: if you're not sure of a word part, think of other words that have the same word part and about what they mean. You can use a dictionary to help you.)

Type of Government	Parts	What the Government is Like
fratocracy	+	
kelptocracy	+	

1. In which type of government does the largest number of people have a say in how the country is run? Fill in the correct circle.

   (a) Communism

   (b) democracy

   (c) oligarchy

2. Complete this analogy:

   a _____

   is to a _____**monarch**_____

   as a _____**dictatorship**_____

   is to a _____ .

3. Look at the phrase in the box below. It's an anagram. Unscramble the letters to spell the name of a famous government leader. Fill in the blanks. An extra letter has already been written in to help you spell the leader's complete name.

   | **LUNCH IS WITH CORN** |

   _ _ _ _ _ _ _

   _ _ _ _ _ _ _ _ _ _ L

4. In a democracy, the people vote for their leaders. On the lines below, write the names of at least three democratic countries.

   _____   _____

   _____

YOUR WORLD

What type of government rules the country in which you live? What do you think is good and bad about it? What do you think it would be like to live in a country that had a different type of government?

- Choose a type of government other than your own, and think about what it would be like to live under it.

- Pretend that you are someone living under this type of government, and write a paragraph about what it's like.

The Middle East

4000–3000 B.C.

- The world's first cities are built by the Sumerian peoples in Mesopotamia, now southern Iraq.
- Sumerians develop a kind of writing called cuneiform.
- Egyptians develop a kind of writing called hieroglyphics.

2700 B.C. Egyptians begin building the great pyramids in the desert. The pharaohs' (kings') bodies are buried in them.

1792 B.C. Some of the first written laws are created in Babylonia. They are called the Code of Hammurabi.

1200 B.C. Hebrew people settle in Canaan in Palestine after escaping from slavery in Egypt. They are led by the prophet Moses.

The Ten Commandments Unlike most early peoples in the Middle East, the Hebrews believed in only one God (monotheism). They believed that God gave Moses the Ten Commandments on Mount Sinai when they fled Egypt.

1200 B.C. King David unites the Hebrews in one strong kingdom.

Ancient Palestine Palestine was invaded by many different peoples after 1000 b.c., including the Babylonians, the Egyptians, the Persians, and the Romans. It came under Arab Muslim control in the 600s and remained mainly under Muslim control until the 1900s.

335 B.C. Alexander the Great, King of Macedonia, builds an empire from Egypt to India.

63 B.C. Romans conquer Palestine and make it part of their empire.

Islam: A Religion Grows in the Middle East 570–632

Muhammad is born in Mecca in Arabia. Around 610, as a prophet, he starts to proclaim and teach Islam, a religion which spreads from Arabia to all the neighboring regions in the Middle East and North Africa. His followers are called Muslims.

632 Muhammad dies. By now, Islam is accepted in Arabia as a religion.

641 Arab Muslims conquer the Persians.

late 600s Islam begins to spread to the west into Africa and Spain.

711–732 Umayyads invade Europe but are defeated by Frankish leader Charles Martel in France. This defeat halts the spread of Islam into Western Europe.

1071 Muslim Turks conquer Jerusalem.

1095–1291 Europeans try to take back Jerusalem and other parts of the Middle East for Christians during the Crusades.

1300–1900s The Ottoman Turks, who are Muslims, create a huge empire, covering the Middle East, North Africa, and part of Eastern Europe. The Ottoman Empire falls apart gradually, and European countries take over portions of it beginning in the 1800s.

1914–1918 World War I begins in 1914. The Ottoman Empire has now broken apart. Most of the Middle East falls under British or French control.

1921 Two new Arab kingdoms are created: Transjordan and Iraq. The French take control of Syria and Lebanon.

1922 Egypt becomes independent from Britain.

Jews Migrate to Palestine

Jewish settlers from Europe began migrating to Palestine in the 1880s. They wanted to return to the historic homeland of the Hebrew people. In 1945, after World War II, many Jews who survived the Holocaust migrated to Palestine. Arabs living in the region opposed the Jewish immigration. In 1948, after the British left, war broke out between the Jews and the Arabs.

1948 The state of Israel is created.

The Arab-Israeli Wars Arab countries near Israel (Egypt, Iraq, Jordan, Lebanon, and Syria) attack the new country in 1948 but fail to destroy it. Israel and its neighbors fight wars again in 1956, 1967, and 1973. Israel wins each war. In the 1967 war, Israel captures the Sinai Desert from Egypt, the Golan Heights from Syria, and the area known as the West Bank from Jordan.

1979 Egypt and Israel sign a peace treaty, providing for Israel to return the Sinai to Egypt.

The 1990s and 2000s

- In 1991, the U.S. and its allies go to war with Iraq after Iraq invades Kuwait. Iraq is defeated and signs a peace agreement but is accused of violating it. In 2003, the U.S. and Britain invade Iraq and remove the regime of Saddam Hussein.
- Tensions between Israel and the Palestinians increase, fueled by suicide bombings by Palestinians, and Israeli military actions in the occupied territories.

Find the following on page 36:

1. a country	2. 23 years after 1922
3. a people	4. a person who ruled
5. a war	6. a religion
7. a type of writing	8. a group of laws

Use words from page 36 to finish the following sentences:

9. _____, who founded the religion of Islam, died in _____ .

10. Israel was created in _____, and it was immediately_____
by five countries.

11. The world's first cities were built by _____ in the land that is now the
country of _____ .

Name the person or people speaking in each question.

12. I led my people into Canaan after we escaped slavery in Egypt.	13. We conquered Palestine in 63 B.C. and added it to our empire.
14. My empire stretched from India to Egypt.	15. I led the army that defeated the Umayyads when they invaded France.

Find three words on page 36 related to each people.

Ottoman Turks	Muslims	Egyptians	Jews

Find the following on page 36:

1. an adjective meaning "extremely large"	2. a synonym for "starts"
3. a noun that rhymes with "fighting"	4. an adverb meaning "slowly and steadily"
5. a preposition that rhymes with "wonder"	6. a contraction meaning "belonging to" or "having to do with" the planet
7. a verb meaning "to attack"	8. an antonym for "stays in one place"

TAKE A CLOSER LOOK

On page 36, we learn that the term *monotheism* means "belief in one god." That is because *mon* or *mono* is a prefix meaning "one" and "the" is a root word meaning "god." In the next paragraph, we see the word *unite*, which means "join together to become one." That is because the prefix *uni* also means "one." Oftentimes two or more prefixes mean the same thing. Look at the chart below of *mono* and *uni* words and their definitions. Add one more of each to the chart.

Prefix	Word	Definition
mono	monotheism	belief in one god
uni	unite	join together to become one
mono		
uni		

1. The great pyramids of Egypt were the burial places of the pharaohs (kings). On page 36, there are two kings mentioned. Although neither was a pharaoh, bury them like they were by writing each of their names in the pyramids below.

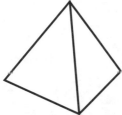 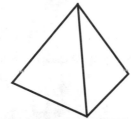

2. Which is not a Muslim people? Fill in the correct circle.

(a) Romans

(b) Jews

(c) Christians

(d) none are a Muslim people

3. The events below are in alphabetical order. Refer to the text on page 36, then put them in chronological order. The first one has been done for you.

Alphabetical Order	Chronological Order
A. Egypt and Israel sign peace treaty	B
B. Egyptians build the great pyramids	
C. Islam founded	
D. Israel founded	
E. Muhammad dies	
F. World War II ends	

4. Use the key in the box to help you figure out the coded words below. When you solve the code, you will have named a territory that existed for about 600 years.

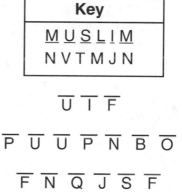

Key
M U S L I M
N V T M J N

U T F

P U U P N B O

F N Q J S F

YOUR WORLD

Have you heard on the news or read in newspapers or magazine stories about the trouble between the Israelis and the Palestinians? The fighting between them has caused problems all over the world, as different countries take different sides in this conflict. There are many in the world who are trying to help these peoples make peace, and they believe there are two choices: 1) a "two-state" solution, in which Israel (who is more in control of the land in the region) allows Palestinians to form their own country with some of the land they live in (the West Bank and/or the Gaza Strip); or 2) the Palestinians are allowed to become Israeli citizens and get the same rights as other Israelis.

- Look at a map of Israel so that you can understand the distribution of the Israelis and the Palestinians.

- Use outside sources (such as the Internet) to read more about the two proposed solutions above.

- Write a paragraph on which of the "solutions" you think is more workable, or come up with an idea that you think would work better.

Native Americans

When European explorers first sailed to North America, they thought they had arrived in the East Indies, near the continent of Asia. That's why the explorers called the people they found living on these lands "Indians."

Scientists now believe that these "American Indians," commonly known today as Native Americans, arrived in the Americas more than 20,000 years ago, most likely from Northeast Asia. Many probably came across from Siberia by a "land bridge" that existed when sea levels were lower. Native Americans are not one people, but many different peoples with their own distinct cultures and traditions.

There were about 850,000 Native Americans living in what is now the United States when Columbus arrived. During the 17th, 18th, and 19th centuries, diseases (including many brought by Europeans) and wars with European settlers and soldiers caused the deaths of thousands of American Indians. As more settlers came, and moved westward, the Native peoples were often displaced. The Indian Removal Act of 1830 allowed the government to force all Indians east of the Mississippi to move to Indian Territory (part of what is now Oklahoma). In 1838 and 1839, in what came to be known as the "Trail of Tears," 16,000 Cherokee Indians in Alabama, Georgia, North Carolina, and Tennessee were moved from their homelands to Indian Territory. Nearly a quarter of them died on the way, of hunger, disease, and cold.

By 1910, there were only about 220,000 Native Americans left in the U.S. In 1924, Congress granted native peoples citizenship. Since then, the American Indian population has increased dramatically. According to the U.S. Census Bureau, the total number of American Indians and Alaska Natives in 2002 was about 2.7 million (not counting people who reported belonging to other ethnic groups in addition to Native American).

Find the following on page 40:

1. a state	2. a year
3. 4,000 x 4 =	4. something you call the day it is right now
5. someone who has a day in October dedicated to him	6. a number between a half-million and a million
7. something you walk across	8. what motivates you to eat

Use words from page 40 to finish the following sentences:

9. It is believed that the people known as Native Americans originally arrived in the Americas more than _____ years ago.

10. In 1830, the U.S. government forced all Native Americans east of the _____ River off their land.

11. Native Americans were originally called _____ because it was thought that the land where they lived was _____ .

Name the state that was part of the "Trail of Tears" based on its abbreviation.

12. NC	13. AL
14. TN	15. GA

Find three words or terms on page 40 related to each aspect of Native American history.

Europeans	"Trail of Tears"	U.S. Government	"Indians"

Find the following on page 40:

1. an antonym for "cold"	2. a noun meaning "fighters" (usually in an army)
3. a homophone of the letter "C"	4. a pronoun meaning "a lot of people"
5. the plural of a compound word meaning "the place a people has lived for a long time"	6. a synonym for "25%"
7. a verb meaning "gotten larger" or "become more"	8. an adverb meaning "notably" or "impressively"

TAKE A CLOSER LOOK

Places are often named after people—or even other places. For example, there are many cities named after Columbus (such as Columbus, Ohio), and the region known as New England (which is the northeast corner of the U.S.) was named after England, which originally colonized it. Look at the places below, guess who or what they are named after, and write down why you think people would want to name a place after that person or place.

Place	What It's Named After	Why
New Mexico		
Washington		

Use the bar graph below to answer questions 1 and 2.

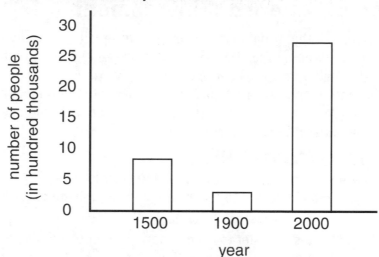

1. In what year (rounded to the nearest hundred) was there the greatest number of Native Americans? Fill in the correct circle.

   (a) 1500

   (b) 1900

   (c) 2000

2. About how many fewer Native Americans were there in the U.S. in 1900 than in 1500? Fill in the correct circle.

   (a) 850,000

   (b) 220,000

   (c) 630,000

Look at the words in the box below. Use them to answer questions #3 and #4.

LOST FAIR RATE

3. The words in the box form an anagram. Unscramble them to find the name given to the harsh, 19th century westward migration of Native Americans in the United States.

   _____

4. About how many Native Americans died during the migration named in question #3? Fill in the correct circle.

   (a) 16,000

   (b) 4,000

   (c) 220,000

YOUR WORLD

Were you born in the place where you live? Were your parents? What about your great-grandparents? Perhaps more than any other people in the world, Americans are a people whose ancestors are often not originally from the land in which they live. Some Americans have Native American ancestors, but this is a very small percentage of the total population.

- Write five questions that you would like to ask a person who was born in another country but now lives in your country. Find a family member or friend who fits this description. Use your questions to interview that person about his or her experiences in a new country.

The U.S. Constitution

The Foundation of American Government

The Constitution is the document that created the present government of the United States. It was written in 1787 and went into effect in 1789. It establishes the three branches of the U.S. government, which are the executive (headed by the president), the legislative (the Congress), and the judicial (the Supreme Court and other federal courts). The first 10 amendments to the Constitution (the **Bill of Rights**) explain the basic rights of all American citizens. You can find the constitution online at: **http://www.house.gov/Constitution/Constitution.html**

The Preamble to the Constitution

The Constitution begins with a short statement called the Preamble. The Preamble states that the government of the United States was established by the people.

"We the people of the United States, in order to form a more perfect union, establish justice, insure domestic tranquility, provide for the common defense, promote the general welfare, and secure the blessings of liberty to ourselves and our posterity, do ordain and establish this Constitution for the United States of America."

THE ARTICLES
The original Constitution contained seven articles. The first three articles of the Constitution establish the three branches of the U.S. government.

Article 1, Legislative Branch Creates the Senate and House of Representatives and describes their functions and powers.

Article 2, Executive Branch Creates the office of the President and the Electoral College and lists their powers and responsibilities.

Article 3, Judicial Branch Creates the Supreme Court and gives Congress the power to create lower courts. The powers of the courts and certain crimes are defined.

Article 4, The States Discusses the relationship of the states to one another and to the citizens. Defines the states' powers.

Article 5, Amending the Constitution Describes how the Constitution can be amended (changed).

Article 6, Federal Law Makes the Constitution the supreme law of the land over state laws and constitutions.

Article 7, Ratifying the Constitution Establishes how to ratify (approve) the Constitution.

The Bill of Rights: *The First Ten Amendments*

1 Guarantees freedom of religion, speech, and the press.
2 Guarantees the right to have firearms.
3 Guarantees that soldiers cannot be lodged in private homes unless the owner agrees.
4 Protects people from being searched or having property searched or taken away by the government without reason.
5 Protects rights of people on trial for crimes.
6 Guarantees people accused of crimes the right to a speedy public trial by jury.
7 Guarantees the right to a trial by jury for other kinds of cases.
8 Prohibits "cruel and unusual punishments."
9 Says specific rights listed in the Constitution do not take away rights that may not be listed.
10 Establishes that any powers not given specifically to the federal government belong to states or the people.

Find the following on page 44:

1. a year	2. a two-digit number
3. a Web site	4. a government leader
5. a place where business people often work	6. a branch of the U.S. government
7. places where trials are held	8. what all U.S. citizens are

Use words from page 44 to finish the following sentences:

9. The beginning of the Constitution is known as the _____.

10. The first 10 _____ of the Constitution are called _____.

11. _____ tells us how to change the Constitution.

Name the article of the Constitution that best covers the issue in each newspaper headline.

12. President Not Sure What His Job Is	13. Constitution Becomes Law
14. Vermont and New Hampshire Argue Over Border	15. Courts Wonder Which One Has Final Say

Find three words or terms on page 44 related to each article of the Constitution.

Article 1	Article 2	Article 3	Article 5

Find the following on page 44:

1. an antonym for "long"	2. a synonym for "freedom"
3. a noun for what tries to stop an opposing team's offense	4. a pronoun meaning "a group of people that includes you"
5. a verb meaning "to put into place for the first time"	6. an four-letter adverb meaning to a greater degree
7. four-syllable noun that is a synonym for "peace"	8. adjective meaning "having to do with the court system"

TAKE A CLOSER LOOK

By looking closely at the word *Preamble* you can tell where it comes in the Constitution. This is because the prefix *pre* means "before." On the other hand, the prefix *post*—as in the word *posterity*—means "after." Look at the chart below of *pre* and *post* words and their definitions. Add one more of each to the chart.

Prefix	Word	Definition
pre	preamble	an introduction to a formal document
post	posterity	coming after; all future generations
pre		
post		

1. When on the time line below—A, B, or C—did the Constitution go into effect? Circle the correct letter.

   1786 ●
   A ●
   1788 ●
   B ●
   1790 ●
   C ●
   1792 ●

2. Which is not part of the executive branch of the U.S. government? Fill in the correct circle.

   (a) Congress

   (b) the president

   (c) the Electoral College

3. Draw lines to match each picture below to the number of the Constitutional Amendment they correspond to.

   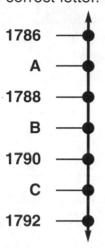

   1ct

   2nd

   3rd

4. Solve this Constitutional riddle:

   I come first, and because of me you can say whatever you want, even if you want to put it in print. What am I?

   _____

   _____

YOUR WORLD

The Constitution established the government of the United States of America, and the U.S. is still governed by it. It may be hard to truly believe, but a document this important in world history was written by people who began by sitting down with a blank piece of paper and putting words on it.

- Read the Preamble of the Constitution.
- Imagine you are among the people founding a new country, and that you have been given the job of writing a short statement of what the principles of your country will be.
- Write your own "Preamble" to this document.

NOBEL PRIZES

The Nobel Prizes are named after Alfred B. Nobel (1833-1896), a Swedish scientist who invented dynamite, and left money for these prizes. They are given every year for promoting peace, and for physics, chemistry, medicine-physiology, literature, and economics.

In 2003, the Peace Prize went to Iranian activist Shirin Ebadi for "her efforts for democracy and human rights." The rights of women and children have been her main concern. She is the first Iranian and first woman from an Islamic country to win it.

PAST WINNERS OF THE NOBEL PEACE PRIZE INCLUDE:

2002 Jimmy Carter, former U.S. president and peace negotiator

2001 United Nations (UN)
Kofi Annan, UN secretary-general

1999 Médecins Sans Frontières (Doctors Without Borders), an organization that gives medical help to disaster and war victims

1997 Jody Williams and the **International Campaign to Ban Landmines**

1994 Yasser Arafat, Palestinian leader

Shimon Peres, foreign minister of Israel

Yitzhak Rabin, prime minister of Israel

1993 Nelson Mandela, leader of South African blacks
F. W. de Klerk, president of South Africa

1992 Rigoberta Menchú Tum, activist for Indian peasant rights in Guatemala

1989 Dalai Lama, Tibetan Buddhist leader, forced into exile in 1959

1986 Elie Wiesel, Holocaust survivor and author

1981 Office of the UN High Commissioner for Refugees

1965 UNICEF (UN Children's Fund)

1964 Martin Luther King Jr., civil rights leader

1961 Dag Hammarskjöld, UN sectretary-general

1919 Woodrow Wilson, U.S. president who played the key role in founding the League of Nations

1906 Theodore Roosevelt, U.S. president who helped settle the Russo-Japanese War

Find the following on page 48:

1. a year	2. a person with awards named after him
3. something people study in school	4. a nationality
5. a war	6. a type of government
7. a government leader	8. a person who has the same name as his father

Use words from page 48 to finish the following sentences:

9. Alfred Nobel was a scientist from _____ who invented _____.

10. In _____, F.W. de Klerk shared the Nobel Peace Prize with

_____.

11. _____ and _____ are two organizations which have won the Nobel Peace Prize.

Name the president based on the clues given:

12. won Nobel Peace Prize some time after 2000	13. League of Nations
14. Russo-Japanese War	15. South Africa

Find three words or terms on page 48 related to each Nobel Prize winner.

Dalai Lama	Nelson Mandela	Rigoberta Menchú Tum	Shirin Ebadi

Find the following on page 48:

1. an antonym for "war"	2. a homophone of a number
3. a proper noun that is also an alliteration	4. an adjective meaning "before any other"
5. a pronoun expressing gender	6. a pronoun that doesn't express gender
7. a prefix meaning "out"	8. an adjective referring to the Muslim religion

TAKE A CLOSER LOOK

People's names in English often don't have any particular meaning, but the name of organizations usually do. However, when we hear the names a lot we may forget what they mean—or never even think about them in the first place. Look at the names of organizations below, then write why you think they have those names.

Organization	Why It's Named What It Is
United Nations	
Doctors without Borders	

1. Look at the time line below. Circle the letter—A, B, or C—that is closest to when Martin Luther King Jr. won the Nobel Peace Prize.

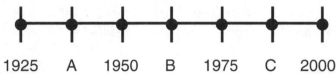

1925   A   1950   B   1975   C   2000

2. Who did not win a Nobel Peace Prize in 1993? Fill in the correct circle.

(a) Yitzhak Rabin   (b) F.W. de Klerk   (c) Nelson Mandela

3. Which symbol does not represent something related to one of the Nobel Prizes that are given out? Fill in the correct circle.

 a

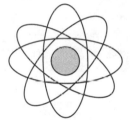

b

c

4. Inside each one of the "Nobel Prizes," write a positive effect that you think giving out the prizes has.

YOUR WORLD

A Nobel Prize is a medallion and a cash amount given each year to recognize excellent work done in the fields of literature, physics, chemistry, medicine/physiology, economics, and promoting peace (one prize in each). If you were in a position to give out an award, what would it be like?

- Draw a design for an award. It can be a medal, a trophy, or whatever you would like to give.

- Also include details of the prize—what it's called, what it recognizes, and why you think it's good to recognize this.

Getting to the Root

Many English words and parts of words can be traced back to Latin or Greek. If you know the meaning of a word's parts, you can probably guess what it means. A **root** (also called a stem) is the part of the word that gives its basic meaning, but can't be used by itself. Roots need other word parts to complete them: either a **prefix** at the beginning, or a **suffix** at the end, or sometimes both. The following tables give some examples of Greek and Latin roots, prefixes, and suffixes.

Latin

root	basic meaning	example
-aqua-	water	aquarium
-ject-	to throw	reject
-mem-	to keep in mind	memory
-port-	to carry	transport
-scrib-/ -script-	to write	prescription

prefix	basic meaning	example
co-	together	cooperate
de-	away, off	defrost
inter-	between, among	international
pre-	before	prevent
re-	again, back	rewrite
sub-	under	subway

prefix	basic meaning	example
-able/-ible	capable or worthy of	workable
-fy/-ify	make or cause to become	horrify
-ly	like, to the extent of	highly
-ous	full of	wondrous
-ty/-ity	state of, power to	purity

Greek

root	basic meaning	example
chron-	time	chronology
-bio-	life	biology
-dem-	people	democracy
-phon-	sound	telephone
-psych-	mind, soul, spirit	psychology
-scope-	to see	telescope

prefix	basic meaning	example
a-/an-	without, not	anaerobic, amoral
auto-	self	autopilot
geo-	Earth	geography
micro-	small	microscope
tele-	far off	television

prefix	basic meaning	example
-ism	act, state, theory of	realism
-ist	one who believes in, practices	capitalist
-graph	write, draw, describe, record	photograph
-logy	talk, speech, study	biology
-meter	measure, measuring device	kilometer

I before **E** except after **C**, or when sounded like **A**, as in **neighbor** or **weigh**.

This is a pretty good rule and helpful in remembering how to spell a lot of words. *Believe, receive,* and *sleigh* are just a few examples. But you do have to learn a few exceptions—cases where the rule doesn't work. The exceptions include *weird, either, neither, height,* and *leisure.*

Find the following on page 52:

1. a language	2. a part of a plant
3. a subject you might study in school	4. a planet
5. something that holds fish	6. something most people watch
7. something you look through	8. something a doctor might write for you

Use words from page 52 to finish the following sentences:

9. The basic meaning of a word comes from its _____ .

10. "Tele-" is a Greek _____ meaning "far off."

11. The word "wondrous" contains the _____ suffix "-ous," which means
    " _____ ."

Find the root of each word. Write the root in the box.

12. remember	13. psychic
14. gramophone	15. antibiotics

Find three words on page 52 related to each part of speech.

Root	Prefix	Suffix

Find the following:

1. a homophone of "C"	2. a prefix meaning "before"
3. a compound word meaning "not having"	4. a verb meaning "to finish"
5. a noun that is something you drink	6. a pronoun which refers to a thing and not a person
7. an adverb meaning "most likely"	8. a synonym for "picture"

TAKE A CLOSER LOOK

Now that we've learned that we put the *E* before the *I* in words like *neighbor* and *weigh*, let's listen to how those words sound. In both words, the *ei* makes a long *a* sound. In English, there are several other ways to make this same sound. In the chart below, give three more ways to make the long *a* sound and provide two examples of each.

Long *a* sound	Example 1	Example 2
ei	neighbor	weigh

Use the chart below to "make" the words necessary to answer questions #1 and #2.

Prefix (Meaning)	Root (Meaning)	Suffix (Meaning)	Suffix (Word Form Created)
in (not, without)	phil (love)	graph (writing)	ic (adjective)
auto (self)	dict (say)	logy (talk, study)	tion (noun)
eu (good)	cred (believe)	form (shape)	er (noun)
mal (bad)	phon (sound)	ible (capable of)	ize (verb)

1. Make a word that describes what you get when you sign your name.

2. You think your friend's band sounds good, and so you decide to make an adjective to describe his music.

----------------------------   ----------------------------

For questions #3 and #4, each object pictured can be broken down into two word parts. Name and define each word part.

3.

Word Part 1:	Word Part 2:
Definition:	Definition:

4.

Word Part 1:	Word Part 2:
Definition:	Definition:

YOUR WORLD

The etymology of a word is the study of where it comes from, of its word parts and development. The etymologies of some words go back literally thousands of years and through several different languages (for example, "democracy" comes originally from Greek origins thousands of years ago and moved through Latin and French), while others come from only one language and much more recently (for example, "rock 'n' roll" was coined by an American radio disc jockey in the 1950s).

- Pick a short paragraph from a book or magazine you like.
- Use a dictionary or the Internet to look up the etymologies of one noun, one verb, and one adjective in the paragraph.
- For each word, make a list of all of the languages and time periods you come across.

Words About Words

An **acronym** is an abbreviation formed from the first letters or syllables of a group of words.	"Radar" comes from "radio detection and ranging"
An **anagram** is a word or phrase made by rearranging the letters from another word or phrase, or perhaps from nonsense letters.	From "Clint Eastwood" you can get the anagram "Old West Action."
Antonyms are words that have opposite meanings.	big and small early and late
A **cliché** is a saying or expression that has been used so often by so many people, it has lost its interest.	She works like a dog. dry as dust
An **eponym** is a word that comes from the name of a person or thing.	"Sandwich" comes from the Earl of Sandwich (1718-1792), who ate these when he was too busy gambling to stop for long.
A **euphemism** is a pleasant word or phrase used in place of a harsher word or phrase.	Instead of "old person": senior citizen Instead of "used car": pre-owned vehicle
Homophones are words that sound alike but have different meanings and spellings.	hear/here hair/hare right/write
A **palindrome** is a word, phrase, or sentence that has exactly the same letters when spelled backward or forward.	no lemons, no melon Ma has a ham.
A **pseudonym** is a name someone makes up and uses to hide his or her true identity.	Daniel Handler, the author of *A Series of Unfortunate Events*, uses the pseudonym "Lemony Snicket."
A **pun** is the use of a word with two different meanings, in a way that's humorous.	The baker said, "I think I'll loaf around all day." Avoidable: What a bullfighter tries to do.
Synonyms are words that have the same or almost the same meanings.	quick and fast tired and sleepy

Find the following on page 56:

1. a food	2. an animal
3. a person	4. a size
5. a profession	6. something you mail
7. an electronic device	8. a number that's not a year

Use words from page 56 to finish the following sentences:

9. The album "The Beatles" is an _____ of the band that recorded it.

10. The words "no" and "_____" are homophones of each other.

11. Not everyone knows that the word "laser" is an _____ for "light amplification by stimulated emission of radiation."

List the "word about words" that there is an example of in each sentence.

12. Mark Twain's real name was Samuel Clemens.	13. That cat is as big as a house.
14. Where will you wear that?	15. "Madam, I'm Adam."

Find three words, phrases, or examples on page 56 related to each "word about words."

Euphemism	Cliché	Acronym	Anagram

Find the following on page 56:

1. an antonym for "same"	2. a noun that means "a group of words"
3. a synonym for "nice"	4. a proper noun
5. a homophone for "weigh"	6. an adjective meaning "a large number"
7. a verb meaning "to possess"	8. an adjective meaning "funny"

TAKE A CLOSER LOOK

A word about words wouldn't be much good if it didn't tell you something about the type of word it describes, would it? But they do. Look at the "words about words" below, break them up into their parts, then write the meaning that comes from those parts. An example has been done for you.

Word About Words	Word Parts	Meanings of Words Parts	Meaning
synonym	syn + nym	alike + name	different words that are alike in what they name
antonym			
pseudonym			
homophone			

1. Which word part does not go with "nym" to form a "word about words"? Fill in the correct circle.

    (a) pseudo

    (b) ant

    (c) palin

2. Unscramble the anagram to reveal the name of one of the most dominant professional basketball players of all time.

    SO ALL HAIL QUEEN

    _____

Below is a list of six "words about words." Read the short paragraph below, and each time you come across an example of something on the list, cross it off. Then answer questions 3 and 4.

acronym   cliché   eponym   homophones (pair)   palindrome   pseudonym

"Look, there's a spaceship on my radar screen."

Sheila put down her sandwich and walked over to his station, bending over his shoulder to look. "I don't see anything.""It's here," Scott pointed, "about two miles out to sea."

"There's nothing there," Sheila replied, annoyed.

"Well, not now. It flew away when it saw me looking at it."

"That's ridiculous," Sheila said, returning to her seat. "They shouldn't allow you around radar."

"Hey," Scott said, "my mother always said that if you can't say something nice, you shouldn't say anything at all."

"I guess I'll just keep quiet then!"

3. Which didn't you cross off? Write your answer here.

    _____

4. On the back of this page, write out the examples of each one of the five that you did cross off.

YOUR WORLD

If you're reading this, at some point in life you acquired language. If you had not been taught language, these symbols you call words and letters would be meaningless to you; and you would not even have any way in which to talk to yourself inside of your own head—let alone out loud to anyone else. Complete the following activity:

- Write a paragraph on what you imagine your experience of existence would be like if you had never acquired language—and yet lived in a world in which language was all around.

All About Books

If a Roman emperor wanted to read a book, he had to unroll it. Books were written on long **scrolls** (kind of like a roll of paper towels) that you unrolled as you went along. This was clumsy, especially if you were looking for a certain passage. Around A.D. 100 the **codex** was invented. It was made up of a stack of pages stitched together at the side and protected by a cover. The codex was easier to carry around, to store, and to search through. Books we read today look something like a codex.

In the Middle Ages books were made by monks who copied them by hand onto prepared animal skins called **parchment**. The monks often decorated the pages with beautiful color illustrations called "illuminations." Books were scarce, and few people who were not priests or monks could read. Even those who could read had to be rich to buy these hand-written books.

A big change came with the use of paper and printing, which were first invented in China. **Paper** came into Europe through the Muslim world and was common by the 14th century. Johann Gutenberg of Germany perfected **printing** in the 1450s. Once books no longer had to be copied by hand and could be printed on paper, they became less expensive and reading became more common.

At first books were still not easy to make and not cheap. Each letter was on a separate piece of type, and a typesetter had to put each piece into place individually. Once all the letters for the page were in place, they were covered with ink and printed, one at a time, by hand on a press. By the 19th century, however, steam-powered presses could print out hundreds of pages at a time. Another invention was the **linotype** machine, which stamped out individual letters and set them up much faster than a typesetter could. Now books had become truly affordable, and the skill of reading was something that everyone was expected to learn.

DID YOU KNOW?

The word "paper" comes from the ancient word "papyrus." Papyrus was a reed used in the ancient world to make writing material. It was made by slicing the stalks and gluing them together in a criss-cross pattern. The sheets were then glued together to make a scroll. Some ancient papyrus scrolls were over 30 feet long.

Find the following on page 60:

1. something in a book	2. a country
3. a place you buy things	4. a political leader
5. a part of your body	6. a historical time period
7. a type of machine	8. something you wipe up spills with

Finish the following sentences:

9. Long before books, people read things off _____, which had to be unrolled to be read.

10. Paper was Invented in _____ over 700 years ago.

11. In the Middle Ages, _____ copied books by hand onto _____.

List the general time period in which each development in book publishing took place.

12. steam-powered presses	13. the codex
14. parchment	15. perfection of printing

Find three words on page 60 related to each part of the history of books.

Monks	Printing	Codex	Typesetting

Find the following on page 60:

1. an adjective that means "major or important"	2. a noun that rhymes with "feasts"
3. a verb meaning "to look for"	4. an antonym for "cheap"
5. an adverb meaning "particularly"	6. a two-word synonym for "pelts"
7. a homophone for the word that comes after "good" when you're leaving someone	8. a compound word meaning "all of us"

TAKE A CLOSER LOOK

Many words in a language are created by putting two words together. This is because over time people find that they have concepts (ideas) they want to communicate that they may not have a word for—but that they can express by putting two already-existing words together. Look at the compound words below. Break them into their parts, then write out their meanings.

Compound Word	Word Parts	Meaning
handwriting		
typeset		

1. Which continent doesn't figure in the development of books? Fill in the correct circle.

   (a) Europe

   (b) Asia

   (c) Antarctica

2. In the word search below, find five terms that are all about books.

I	N	K	P	K	L	E	E
S	T	E	R	N	A	P	T
C	O	D	E	X	A	P	I
R	E	A	S	L	S	A	V
O	U	R	S	T	E	G	R
L	O	O	F	X	L	E	S
L	N	M	K	W	A	S	C
S	I	I	O	S	L	E	N

3. Complete this analogy:

   _____ is to the

   present day

   as **parchment** is to

   _____

4. There are many people who believe that reading and the development of books is the most important development in human history. On the cover of each of the three books below, write down a reason why you think books were important in advancing human civilization.

YOUR WORLD

Because of technology, today the world is connected more than ever before. You can turn on the television and see video footage from halfway across the world; you can jump online and chat with people from several different countries at once; you can climb aboard a jet plane and be most anywhere on Earth in a matter of hours. But even before these modern inventions, people of one culture would often influence others far away—it just happened much more slowly. This is what happened in the development of books.

- Using an outside source (such as *The World Almanac*), make a simple map that includes all of the places referred to on page 60 (including Ancient Rome and "the Muslim world").

- On the map, write out where and when the various developments in printing occurred and how they spread from one place to another (such as printing being invented in China and moving throughout the Muslim world to Europe).

COMPUTER TALK

BIT The smallest unit of data.

BLOG is short for "Web log." It's a personal journal or diary that people put on a website for others to read.

BOOKMARK A feature in web browsers that lets the user save a favorite website. It can be used instead of typing in the URL.

BOOT To start up a computer.

BROWSER A program to help get around the Internet.

BUG OR GLITCH An error in a program or in the computer.

BYTE An amount of data equal to 8 bits.

CHIP A small piece of silicon holding the circuits used to store and process information.

COOKIE Some websites store information, like your passwords and other preferences, on your computer's hard drive. When you go back to that site later, your browser sends the information (the "cookie") to the website.

DATABASE A large collection of information organized so that it can be retrieved and used in different ways.

DESKTOP PUBLISHING The use of computers to design and produce magazines, newspapers, and books.

DOWNLOAD To transfer information from a host computer to a personal computer, often through a modem.

ENCRYPTION The process of changing information into a code, especially passwords, or financial or personal information, to keep others from reading it.

GIG OR GIGABYTE (GB) An amount of information equal to 1,024 megabytes.

HACKER A computer expert who likes to look at the code of operating systems and other programs to see how they work. Some hackers tamper with other people's information and programs illegally.

HTML The abbreviation for HyperText Markup Language, a computer language used to make web pages.

INTERNET A worldwide system of linked computer networks.

K Stands for kilo, or "thousands," in Greek. Used to represent bytes of data or memory.

MEGABYTE (MB) An amount of information equal to 1,048,516 bytes.

NETWORK A group of computers linked together so that they can share information.

PDA OR PERSONAL DIGITAL ASSISTANT A handheld computer that can store addresses, phone numbers, and other information that's useful to have handy.

PIXEL OR PICTURE ELEMENT The smallest unit of an image on a computer monitor. It can be used to measure the size of an image.

PORTAL A website that serves as a gateway to the Internet.

RAM OR RANDOM ACCESS MEMORY Memory your computer uses to open programs and store your work until you save it to a hard drive or disk. Information in RAM disappears when the computer is turned off.

ROM OR READ ONLY MEMORY Memory that contains permanent instructions for the computer and cannot be changed. The information in ROM stays after the computer is turned off.

SPAM Electronic junk mail.

THREAD A series of messages and replies that relate to a specific topic.

URL OR UNIFORM RESOURCE LOCATOR The technical name for a website address.

VIRUS A program that damages other programs and data. It gets into a computer through telephone lines or shared disks.

WI-FI OR WIRELESS FIDELITY Technology that allows people to link to other computers and the Internet from their computers without wires.

Computer Talk

Find the following on page 64:

1. what a spider makes	2. something sweet to eat
3. reading material	4. a Greek word
5. something you talk into	6. a homophone for something you might get from a group of mosquitoes
7. a homonym for a kind of meat that comes in a can	8. something that makes you sick

Use words from page 64 to finish the following sentences:

9. _____ is the changing of information into code.

10. The information in RAM (random access memory) _____ once you turn your computer off.

11. A _____ is the _____ part of an image on a computer monitor.

Write out what each acronym stands for.

12. ROM	13. RAM
14. PDA	15. HTML

Find three words on page 64 related to each bit of computer talk.

Internet	Chip	Bookmark	Cookie

Find the following on page 64:

1. an antonym for "soft"	2. an abbreviation for "1,000"
3. a compound word meaning "to transfer information from one computer to another"	4. a superlative meaning "the least in size"
5. a noun that rhymes with "liar"	6. a verb meaning "to hold or retain"
7. a prefix meaning "between" or "among"	8. a word root meaning "secret"

TAKE A CLOSER LOOK

Nouns are often made out of the thing that they do. A runner is someone who runs, a compact disc (CD) player is something that plays compact discs. Look at nouns below and name the action that they are named for, then write out an appropriate definition—one that doesn't use the noun's root verb.

Noun	Action It Comes from	Meaning
browser		
hacker		

1. Which picture doesn't represent a homonym of a computer term? Fill in the correct circle.

ⓐ　　　ⓑ　　　ⓒ

2. A piece of information has come your way in an encrypted form. Use the example to crack the code and fill in the hidden computer term.

If 2 • 9 • 20 = BIT

then 16 • 15 • 18 • 20 • 1 • 12 =

3. Fill in the computer talk word chain. Each word must begin with either the first or last letter of either the word before it or after it.

GLITCH
H _ _ _ _ _ _
ROM
_ _ _ _ _ _ _ _ E
_ _ _ _ _ _ _ _ _ N
ERROR
B _ _ _ _ _ _ _
_ _ _ _ G

4. Unscramble the anagram below to find a term that is computer talk for an amount of information, then write out its definition.

boy like T

Word: _____

Definition: _____

_____

_____

YOUR WORLD

Have you used a computer? Do you own a computer? Computers are so common today that it may have seemed like they've been around for a long time, but that's just not true. Consider this: the personal computer you have at home—even if it's not brand new—has more computing power and speed than the computer NASA had when they first put a man on the moon. Choose one of the following activities:

- write a paragraph about why you think computers have become so popular; or
- create something on a computer that showcases several different aspects of computer technology

Calendar Basics

Holidays and calendars go hand in hand. Using a calendar, you can see what day of the week it is, and watch out for the next special day. Calendars divide time into days, weeks, months, and years. A year is the time it takes for one revolution of Earth around the Sun. Early calendars were lunar—based on the movements of the Moon across the sky. The ancient Egyptians were probably the first to develop a solar calendar, based on the movements of Earth around the Sun.

THE JULIAN AND GREGORIAN CALENDARS

In 46 B.C., the emperor Julius Caesar decided to use a calendar based on movements of the Sun. This calendar, called the **Julian calendar**, fixed the normal year at 365 days and added one day every fourth year (leap year). It also established the months of the year and the days of the week.

Pope Gregory XIII revised the Julian calendar in A.D. 1582 because the year was 11 minutes, 14 seconds too long. This added up to about 3 extra days every 400 years. To fix it, he made years ending in 00 leap years only if they can be divided by 400. Thus, 2000 was a leap year, but 2100 will not be. The **Gregorian calendar** is the one used today in most of the world.

JEWISH, ISLAMIC, AND CHINESE CALENDARS

The Jewish calendar, which began almost 6,000 years ago, is the official calendar of Israel. The year 2004 is the same as 5764–5765 on the Jewish calendar, which starts at Rosh Hashanah, usually in September. The Islamic calendar started in a.d. 622. The year 2004 is equivalent to 1424–1425 on the Islamic calendar, which begins with the month of Muharram, usually in February or March. The Chinese calendar has years named after animals. There are 12 of them: Rat, Ox, Tiger, Rabbit, Dragon, Snake, Horse, Sheep, Monkey, Rooster, Dog, and Pig. On January 22, 2004, the Year of the Monkey began. On February 9, 2005, the Year of the Rooster starts.

BIRTHSTONES

MONTH	BIRTHSTONE
January	Garnet
February	Amethyst
March	Aquamarine
April	Diamond
May	Emerald
June	Pearl
July	Ruby
August	Peridot
September	Sapphire
October	Opal
November	Topaz
December	Turquoise

THE NAMES OF THE MONTHS

January	named for the Roman god Janus, guardian of gates (often shown with two faces, looking backward and forward)
February	named for Februalia, a Roman time of sacrifice
March	named for Mars, the Roman god of war (the end of winter meant fighting could begin again)
April	"aperire," Latin for "to open," as in flower buds
May	named for Maia, the goddess of plant growth
June	"Junius," the Latin word for the goddess Juno
July	named after the Roman ruler Julius Caesar
August	named for Augustus, the first Roman emperor
September	"septem," the Latin word for seven
October	"octo," the Latin word for eight
November	"novem," the Latin word for nine
December	"decem," the Latin word for ten

Find the following on page 68:

1. a year	2. a birthstone
3. an animal	4. a Roman numeral
5. a planet other than Earth	6. a three-digit number
7. a Latin word that is not a name	8. a calendar named after a person

Use words from page 68 to finish the following sentences:

9. The _____ calendar is almost 1,000 years older than the _____ calendar.

10. Calendars now are based on _____ moving around the sun, while the earliest calendars were based on the movements of _____.

11. The Julian calendar was revised by _____ in _____ because the year was too long.

Name the month indicated by each clue.

12. ruby	13. Janus
14. the Latin word for "nine"	15. something made by oysters

Calendar Basics   Vocabulary Hunt

Find three words on page 68 related to each calendar.

Islamic	Chinese	Julian	Gregorian

Find the following on page 68:

1. a number that is a palindrome	2. a synonym for the word "jump"
3. a three-word adverb meaning "earlier" or "in the past"	4. an antonym for "ordinary"
5. a noun whose only consonant is "X"	6. a prefix meaning "water"
7. a verb ending in "-ed" that means "separated or cut apart"	8. a four-syllable adjective meaning "the same as"

========= **TAKE A CLOSER LOOK** =========

On the Gregorian calendar, it is easy to see where the months get their names. However, it is not always the case that what something is named after is easy to see in the name. Look at the days of the week below. Guess how each one got its name, then use a dictionary to find out where it came from. Did you find anything that surprised you?

Day of the Week	Your Guess About Its Name	What It's Named After
Sunday		
Monday		

1. Solve the following math problem:

    (septem plus decem)

    minus octo

    equals

    _____.

2. Fill in the time line of calendar history:

    about
    4,000 B.C.   ● _____

    46 B.C.   ● _____

    A.D. 622   ● _____

    A.D. 1582   ● _____

3. Unscramble the string of letters to find a month that begins the year:

    HUAARRMM

    _____

4. Complete this analogy:

    _____ is to

    the Jewish calendar

    as New Year's Day

    is to _____.S

YOUR WORLD

As you can see from what you've now read about calendars, they can be based on different things, and the months and years can be broken up in many different ways. Why does the Chinese calendar rotate in 12-year cycles? Why is September the ninth month on the Gregorian calendar even though it gets its name from the Latin word for *seven*? Why do different calendars begin their years at different times?

*   Using an outside source such as *The World Almanac* or an encyclopedia, try to get an idea about the different ways in which calendars are set up.
*   Then, on a separate sheet of paper, design your own calendar, coming up with your own reasoning behind how you're breaking up your days and months and how you're naming them.

The Metric System

The metric system was created in France in 1795. Standardized in 1960 and given the name International System of Units, it is now used in most countries. The system is based on 10, like the decimal counting system. The basic unit for length is the meter. The liter is a basic unit of volume or capacity, and the gram is a basic unit of mass. Related units are made by adding a prefix to the basic unit. The prefixes and their meanings are:

milli- = 1/1,000   deci- = 1/10   hecto- = 100

centi- = 1/100   deka- = 10   kilo- = 1,000

FOR EXAMPLE:

millimeter (mm) = 1/1,000 of a meter   milligram (mg) = 1/1,000 of a gram

kilometer (km) = 1,000 meters   kilogram (kg) = 1,000 grams

To get a rough idea of measurements in the metric system, it helps to know that a liter is a little more than a quart. A meter is a little over a yard. A kilogram is a little over 2 pounds. And a kilometer is just over half a mile.

Converting Measurements

From:	Multiply by:	To get:	From:	Multiply by:	To get:
inches	2.5400	centimeters	centimeters	.3937	inches
inches	.0254	meters	centimeters	.0328	feet
feet	30.4800	centimeters	meters	39.3701	inches
feet	.3048	meters	meters	3.2808	feet
yards	.9144	meters	meters	1.0936	yards
miles	1.6093	kilometers	kilometers	.621	miles
square inches	6.4516	square centimeter	square centimeters	.1550	square inches
square feet	.0929	square meters	square meters	10.7639	square feet
square yards	.8361	square meters	square meters	1.1960	square yards
acres	.4047	hectares	hectares	2.4710	acres
cubic inches	16.3871	cubic centimeters	cubic centimeters	.0610	cubic inches
cubic feet	.0283	cubic meters	cubic meters	35.3147	cubic feet
cubic yards	.7646	cubic meters	cubic meters	1.3080	cubic yards
quarts (liquid)	.9464	liters	liters	1.0567	quarts (liquid)
ounces	28.3495	grams	grams	.0353	ounces
pounds	.4536	kilograms	kilograms	2.2046	pounds

Find the following on page 72:

1. a fraction	2. a word in boldface type
3. a year	4. a number with numerals on both sides of a decimal point
5. the name of a shape	6. an amount of liquid that is a little more than a quart
7. a word for a part of speech	8. 100 divided by 1/100 =

Use words from page 72 to finish the following sentences:

9. The metric system was _____ in 1960, but it was created in _____ .

10. A yard is a little _____ than a meter, and a _____ is a little longer than a half-mile.

11. About 56.7 _____ is the equivalent of _____ ounces.

Translate each amount into a one-word metric term.

12. 1/1000 of a meter	13. 1/10 of a meter
14. 1/100 of a liter	15. 100 grams

Find three metric terms on page 72 related to each type of measurement.

Length	Weight	Area	Volume

Find the following on page 72:

1. a prefix meaning "10"	2. an abbreviation for kilogram
3. a proper noun	4. an antonym for "smooth"
5. an adjective meaning "the majority of"	6. a synonym for "fundamental"
7. a five-letter word with the first, third, and fifth letters of the alphabet	8. a type of measurement that is an alliteration

TAKE A CLOSER LOOK

You've probably noticed that, no matter what type of measurement you're doing, the prefixes of the metric system stay the same. With these prefixes in mind, in the spaces below, create a metric-sounding word that would match the length of time you're asked to describe (for example, 1/100 of a day would be a *centiday*). Then see if you can come up with an English word that is also a good description. What do you notice when you compare the word you came up with the English word?

Amount	Your "Metric" Word	English Word	What You Notice
a 10-year period			
a 100-year period			
a 1,000-year period			

1. Solve the following conversion problem:

   6.21 miles =

   _____ kilometers

   = _____ meters.

2. Measure Line A below with a ruler that measures in inches. Then convert this measurement to metric. How many centimeters is the line?

   _____

   |——————————————————————|
   Line A

3. If it takes Greggory 13 seconds to run 100 yards and it takes Eric the same amount of time to run 100 meters, who is faster? Fill in the correct circle.

   (a) Greggory   (b) Eric

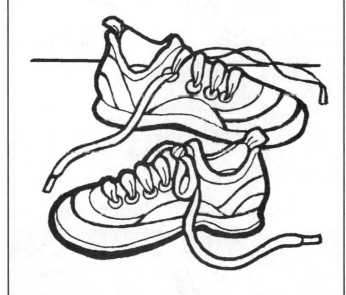

4. Imagine that you are the coach of an expansion NBA franchise called the Montana Metrics, and that you can draft any players who ever played in the NBA—with one catch: each player you draft must have initials that match up with a metric abbreviation. From the list of all-time greats below, which ones can you draft?

   Kareem Abdul-Jabbar   Michael Jordan

   Allen Iverson   Jerry West

   Kevin Garnett   Dennis Rodman

   Julius Erving   Wilt Chamberlain

   Michael Jordan   Moses Malone

   Larry Bird   "Magic" Johnson

   Rick Barry   Shaquille O'Neal

   Karl Malone

YOUR WORLD

In the 1970s, there was a movement in the United States to replace the country's system of measurements with the metric system. However, aside from a few exceptions, the movement failed, because Americans didn't want to learn a new (to them) system. Write a paragraph taking one of the following positions:

- Americans should convert to the metric system. Be sure to talk about the benefits of the new system, etc.
- Americans should keep its current system. Talk about what's better about this system or the problems with changing to a new system, etc.

Money Around the World

When you go to a foreign country, one of the first things you may notice is what the money looks like. Many countries have colorful bills in different shapes and sizes. They often show queens or presidents or other famous people. But you also may find a rhinoceros, tiger, or elephant (India), a sea turtle (Brazil), cows and fruit (Nigeria), a map of the North Pole (Norway), or even schoolchildren (Taiwan).

All About...The Euro

There are now 25 members of the European Union (10 of them joined in May 2004). Twelve of them now all have the same currency—all their coins and paper money are Euros. Now all have the same currency; all their coins and paper money are **euros**. The euro is used in Austria, Belgium, Finland, France, Germany, Greece, Ireland, Italy, Luxembourg, the Netherlands, Portugal, and Spain. The one-euro coin is now a common sight. The front (**obverse**) side of the coin has the word "euro" and a map of the euro area. On the other side (**reverse**), each euro country has a national symbol, such as the Irish harp for Ireland, and a portrait of the king for Spain.

People in France and Italy miss their francs and lire. But now money flows easily from one country to another. This makes it easier to complete big financial deals between countries. And tourists can use the same kind of money to pay for a slice of pizza whether it's in Italy or in Belgium.

The euro has been increasing in value in comparison to the dollar. This makes it more expensive for Americans to go to Europe! The euro was worth about $1.22 in spring 2004.

What Are Exchange Rates?

When one country exports goods to another, the payment from the country buying the goods must be changed into the currency of the country selling them. People traveling to other countries usually need to convert their money into the local currency. In some countries, like Canada, stores will accept U.S. money for purchases, but will give change in Canadian money. How do they know how much change to give you? An exchange rate—that gives the price of one currency in terms of another—is used. For example, in March 2004 one U.S. dollar could buy 1.22 Canadian dollars.

Here are the exchange rates in 1990 and 2004 between the U.S. dollar and the currency of some of the country's biggest trading partners.

What A U.S. Dollar Bought

COUNTRY	IN 1990	IN 2004
Canada	1.2 Canadian dollars	1.34 Canadian dollars
Great Britain (UK)	0.56 pound	0.56 pound
European Union*	—	1.22 euros
Japan	144.8 yen	110.8 yen
Mexico	2.8 pesos	10.96 pesos

*The euro is used in twelve countries of the European Union (see above). Three longtime members of the union do not use the euro: Great Britain, Denmark, and Sweden.

76

Money Around the World   Content Hunt

Find the following on page 76

1. a country	2. a continent
3. a word in quotation marks	4. $2 − .78 =
5. a season	6. a number that is spelled out
7. another name for Great Britain	8. a word with the 26th letter of the alphabet twice in a row

Use words from page 76 to finish the following sentences:

9. Twelve members of the _____ all have the same currency, which is called the _____.

10. Both _____ and _____ call their basic unit of money the dollar—even though they're worth different amounts.

11. _____ are how people know how to convert the money from one country into the money of another.

Name the basic form of money that is used by each country.

12. Mexico	13. Japan
14. the Netherlands	15. France

Find three words on page 76 related to each aspect of the world of money.

Euro	Animals	Coins	Exchange Rates

Find the following on page 76:

1. the initials of the European Union	2. a proper noun that begins and ends with the same letter
3. a noun rhyming with "peace"	4. a pronoun meaning a group of people not including yourself
5. a verb meaning to possess or own	6. a suffix meaning most
7. a synonym for "costly"	8. a two-letter preposition starting with a vowel

TAKE A CLOSER LOOK

Many words in language are shortened versions of longer words or combinations of words. For example, "America" is a shortened version of "the United States of America"—because not only are there other countries in North America, there is a whole other continent with "America" in its name: South America. Look at the terms below, and where you think the terms come from.

Term	Hint	Where the Term Comes from
euro	place	
Benelux	combination of 3 countries	

1. Which is worth more (based on 2004 exchange rates)? Fill in the correct circle.

    (a) one pound

    (b) one Canadian dollar

    (c) one U.S. dollar

    (d) all worth the same

2. Which is worth more (based on 2004 exchange rates)? Fill in the correct circle.

    (a) 1.34 Canadian dollars

    (b) 1.22 euros

    (c) 110.8 yen

    (d) all worth the same

3. Look at the graph of exchange rates between the U.S. dollar and the peso. Based on the exchange rates, in which month would it be the least expensive for an American to go to Mexico? Which month would be the most expensive?

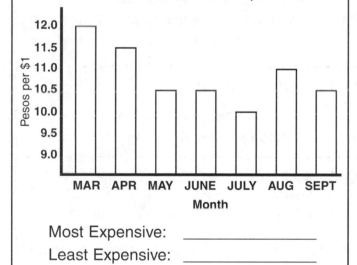

Month

Most Expensive: _____

Least Expensive: _____

4. Three longtime members of the European Union do not use the euro. Next to each picture, write the name of an EU country that doesn't use the euro.

  _____

  _____

  _____

YOUR WORLD

When a country has its own money, it puts things on the money that have to do with that country. In the U.S., for example, the money has things on it like former presidents and major U.S. landmarks. When the 12 countries in the European Union decided to have a common money, they had to decide on designs that they could all agree on. Pretend that two or more countries nearest yours have decided to use a common money—and that you have been chosen to design it. Pick one denomination (such as the one-euro coin), and draw it.

*   Be sure to come up with a design that represents each country equally and fairly, as well as something that reflects the union of the countries involved.

*   Whether it's a coin or a bill, don't forget to put something on both sides.

Percents and Fractions

The term *percent* means *per hundred*. 10 percent (10%) means 10 out of a hundred, or $^{10}/_{100}$, or 10 divided by 100.

Let's say you had 100 marbles, and you gave some to a friend. What percent of the marbles did you give away? If you gave away 10 marbles, that would be 10 out of 100, or 10%. But that is an easy number to use. What if you had 300 marbles, and gave away 72? What percent of the 300 marbles did you give away? What fraction?

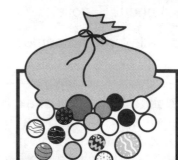

To calculate the percentage,

- divide 72 by 300.
- $72 \div 300 = .24 = 24$ hundredths = $^{24}/_{100}$.
- Since percent means per hundred, "24 per 100" = 24%.

To go from a percentage to a fraction,
- divide the percentage by 100 then reduce the fraction.

First rename 24% to $^{24}/_{100}$. Then reduce that fraction to its lowest common denominator. You do this by dividing both the numerator (the top number) and the denominator (the bottom number) by the largest number by which both can be divided. In this case that number is 4. So $^{24}/_{100} = ^{6}/_{25}$.

Fractals: Painting by Numbers

Did you know that mathematicians can paint pictures with numbers? The French mathematician Benoit Mandelbrot did this in 1975 when he discovered fractals. Fractals are never-ending patterns of self-repeating shapes created by graphing different algebraic equations. These colorful pictures are made up of patterns of geometric shapes (like circles and squares, but more complex), which can be broken down into smaller sizes, down to a microscopic level. Many things in nature are fractal in structure. That's why scientists can use fractal geometry to make models of coastlines, mountains, and even the shapes of clouds!

Searching for Prime Numbers

Mathematicians have long been interested in prime numbers. A prime number is any number bigger than 1 that can't be divided without a remainder—except by itself and 1.

So 2 would be a prime number. But it's the only even number that's a prime, since every even number can be divided by 2.

3 is another prime number. Can you figure out which other numbers under 10 would be prime numbers? How about from 20 to 30? (If you can't tell right away, try dividing by odd numbers starting with 3. If nothing works, you've got a prime.)

How many prime numbers are there? An infinite number! And mathematicians using computers have figured out prime numbers higher than you could imagine.

Find the following on page 80:

1. a percentage	2. a single-digit number
3. a year	4. a profession
5. something you can see on a globe	6. 10% of 720 =
7. a nationality	8. a denominator

Use words from page 80 to finish the following sentences:

9. A _____ number can be divided only by 1 and _____ without there being a remainder.

10. _____ is a good mathematical tool to use numbers to make models of clouds.

11. You turn the fraction 5/10 into 1/2 by _____ it to its_____.

Find each answer based on the information given.

12. a never-ending pattern of a self-repeating shape	13. the "38" in the fraction 38/99
14. the only even prime number	15. 80% as a reduced fraction

Primes, Percents, Fractions, & Fractals   Vocabulary Hunt

Find three words on page 80 related to each aspect of math.

Primes	Percents	Fractions	Fractals

Find the following on page 80:

1. a verb that rhymes with "live"	2. a proper noun
3. a prefix meaning "very small"	4. a contraction for two words, one of which is "us"
5. a word beginning with a vowel that can be a noun, adjective, or adverb	6. a noun meaning "framework" or "form"
7. an adjective ending in "ic"	8. a synonym for "never-ending"

TAKE A CLOSER LOOK

The words of all languages are derived (come) from earlier versions of that language and/or from other, often earlier, languages—and this may be more true of English than of any other language. For example, the word "percent" is a combination of the Latin words *per* (by) and *cent* (hundred). Look at the two words below. What do they have in common? Re-read page 80, then define each of these words based on what word root they share.

Word	What They Have in Common	Definition
fraction		
fractal		

Primes, Percents, Fractions, & Fractals Hodgepodge Hunt

1. Which section of the pie chart is more than 60%? Shade in the correct section.

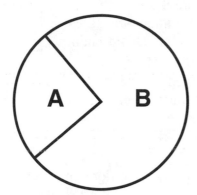

2. Which is the smallest amount? Fill in the correct circle.

   (a) 22%

   (b) 22/80

   (c) 1/8

3. The letters below once formed two words that are different ways of representing the same thing. Those letters have been broken into groups and rearranged. Put them back in the right order to find the two words.

   ONS FR AC EN TS PE RC TI

   Word 1: _____

   Word 2: _____

4. Just because most numbers *aren't* prime numbers doesn't mean that we don't use prime numbers a lot. Look at the prime numbers below and write one way we encounter these numbers in our everyday life. The first one has been done for you.

   7 = <u>number of days in a week</u>

   11 = _____

   31 = _____

YOUR WORLD

Most people know who Albert Einstein is, but how many other scientists can you name? We live in a world in which sports stars, musicians, and movie stars are often known by millions of people, but scientists by very few—even though what *they* do often transforms the very world in which we live!

- Using a source like *The World Almanac* or an encyclopedia, read about a scientist you've never heard of.
- Then, write a paragraph on what that scientist did that changed some aspect of the world—and why he or she is worth knowing about.

Finding the Area

Finding the area of a figure can be easy, if you know the not-so-secret formula.

AREA OF A SQUARE:

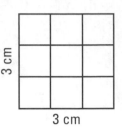

A plane figure with four sides is called a **quadrilateral**. A square is a quadrilateral with four right angles and four equal sides, like the figure you see here. To find the area for a square, use this formula: **side x side** (**side x side** can also be written as S^2, pronounced "side squared").

The sides of this square are each 3 centimeters long. So the area is 3 x 3, or 9. These are no longer centimeters but **square centimeters**, like the smaller squares inside the big one.

AREA OF A RECTANGLE:

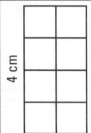

Rectangles are another type of quadrilateral. They have four right angles, but unlike a square, the sides are not all equal.

To find the area of a rectangle, multiply **BASE x HEIGHT** (length x width).

This rectangle has a base of 4 centimeters and a height of 2 centimeters. Its area is 8 square centimeters.

AREA OF A PARALLELOGRAM:

Parallelograms are quadrilaterals that have parallel opposite sides, but no right angles. The formula for the area of a parellelogram is the same as a rectangle—**BASE x HEIGHT.**

AREA OF A TRIANGLE:

A triangle is a three-sided plane figure. The prefix "tri" means three, which refers to the three points where the sides of a triangle meet.

To find the area for a triangle use **1/2 x (BASE x HEIGHT)** (first multiply the base by the height, then multiply that number by 1/2).

This triangle has a base of 2 centimeters and a height of 3 centimeters. So the area will be 3 square centimeters.

AREA OF A CIRCLE:

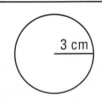

The distance around a circle is called its **circumference**. All the points on the circumference are an equal distance from the center. That distance is the **radius.** A **diameter** is any straight line that has both ends on the circle and passes through its center. It's twice as long as the radius.

To find the circle's area you need to use π—a number called **pi** (π) that equals about 3.14.

The formula for area is: π **x RADIUS X RADIUS** (or π **x RADIUS SQUARED**)

For instance, this circle has a radius of 3 centimeters, so its area = π x 3 x 3, or about $\pi \times 3^2$; that is, 3.14 x 9. This comes to 28.26 square centimeters.

What is Pi? The Greek letter pi (π) stands for the number you get when you divide the circumference of a circle by its diameter. It is always the same, no matter how big the circle is! The Babylonians discovered this in 2000 b.c. Actually, no one can say exactly what the value of π is. When you divide the circumference by the diameter it does not come out even, and you can keep going as many places as you want: 3.14159265…it goes on forever.

Find the following on page 84:

1. a shape	2. a word in *italics*
3. a year	4. a fraction
5. a number that is spelled out	6. a Greek letter
7. a number with two digits on each side of the decimal place	8. a people

Use words from page 84 to finish the following sentences:

9. If you want to find the area of a parallelogram, multiply its _____ by its _____.

10. A square is a type of _____ with four equal sides and four _____.

11. All points on the _____ of a circle are an equal distance from its _____.

Look at the form of each equation, then determine which shape's area is being calculated.

12. 1/2 (8 cm x 6 cm)	13. 8 cm x 6 cm
14. 8 cm^2	15. 3.14 x 14 cm^2

Find three words on page 84 related to each aspect of the measurement of area.

Quadrilateral	Squared	Base	Pi

Find the following on page 84:

1. a prefix meaning three	2. a hyphenated three-word phrase
3. a synonym for "discover"	4. a prefix meaning "four"
5. an adjective meaning "different from"	6. a three-letter article
7. a word that can be a direction, an angle, or mean "correct"	8. a homophone for an antonym of "fancy"

TAKE A CLOSER LOOK

The names of shapes can often have roots that tell you something about the shape they describe. For example, "triangle" means "three angles" ("tri-" + "angle"). Break the words below into their separate parts, then write what the parts tell you.

Shape	Word Parts	What They Tell You
parallelogram		
rectangle		

1. What is the area of the square? Write your answer on the line below.

10 mi.

_____

2. Which of the shapes below has the greatest area? Fill in the a, b, or c bubble to answer the question.

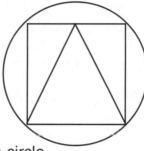

ⓐ　the circle
ⓑ　the square
ⓒ　the triangle

3. Inside each one of the shapes below, write a reason somebody might need to know how to calculate an area of that shape.

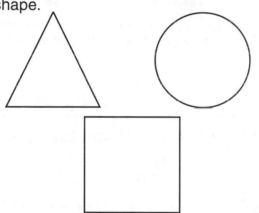

4. Look at the two identical triangles below. What two other shapes can you make using them? Write your answers on the lines below.

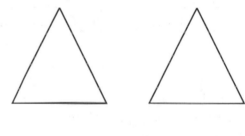

_____
_____

YOUR WORLD

Every two-dimensional surface ever made has a definite area—and now you have the know-how to calculate it! That's a good thing, too, because you're about to practice.

- Find the area of these two-dimensional (flat) surfaces: the top of your textbook and the top of your desk.

  - First, locate on page 84 the proper equation to find the area.

  - Using a measuring device, make the necessary measurements.

  - Plug in the numbers, do the equation, and write down the area of these two objects.

Through Artists' Eyes

Artists look at the world in a new way. Their work can be funny or sad, beautiful or disturbing, real-looking or strange.

Throughout history, artists have painted pictures of nature (called **landscapes**), pictures of people (called **portraits**), and pictures of flowers in vases, food, and other objects (known as **still lifes**). Today many artists create pictures that do not look like anything in the real world. These are examples of **abstract art**, or modern art.

Photography, too, may be a form of art. Photos record both the commonplace and the exotic, and help us look at events in new ways.

Sculpture is a three-dimensional form made from clay, stone, metal, or other material. Sculptures can be large, like the Statue of Liberty, or small. Some are real-looking. Others have no form you can recognize.

PAINTING ON *WALLS*

If you drew on the walls when you were a little kid, you probably got into trouble. But did you know you were following a tradition thousands of years old? Humans have drawn and painted on walls for at least 17,000 years! Prehistoric people used earth pigments and animal fat to create animal scenes on walls of their caves. The most famous of these cave paintings today were discovered in 1940 in a cave near Lascaux in France.

Frescoes are another type of wall painting. They are made by painting on fresh, wet plaster. The most famous fresco in history was done by Michelangelo when Pope Julius II gave him the job of repainting the ceiling of the Sistine Chapel with scenes from the Bible. It took years for him to finish this masterpiece (1508–1512), which he painted lying on his back on a scaffold. You can still see his work today if you travel to Rome and visit the Vatican; in fact, it was recently restored to look just as it did when Michelangelo finished it.

Some murals today are aimed mainly at brightening a neighborhood. Others are done to remember special people or events. You don't need to be famous to paint on walls. You could join a community group that paints (with permission) on walls or the sides of buildings. Murals are a kind of art that is for the people and by the people.

Find the following on page 88:

1. a year	2. a famous statue
3. a city	4. what you eat
5. a book	6. what a joke is supposed to be
7. something people keep in albums	8. what we are

Use words from page 88 to finish the following sentences:

9. There are cave paintings that are at least _____ years old.

10. Landscapes are paintings of _____, while portraits are paintings of _____.

11. _____ painted a _____ on the ceiling of the Sistine Chapel.

Name the artform that is *most* related to the materials listed.

12. camera, lens	13. brushes, canvas
14. clay, stone	15. earth pigments, animal fat

Find three words on page 88 related to each artform.

Painting	Sculpture	Fresco	Mural

Find the following on page 88:

1. a synonym for "planet"	2. a prefix meaning "before"
3. an antonym for "big"	4. a contraction
5. an anagram for the word "straits"	6. an adverb meaning "also"
7. a compound word meaning something truly great	8. a noun meaning "custom"

TAKE A CLOSER LOOK

There are many words that have both noun and verb forms that mean very close to the same thing. Think of the word "flash." You can say, "Use the flash [noun] so that there'll be enough light for the picture"; and also, "Flash [verb] that light over here." Look at the words below, then tell what each means as a noun and as a verb.

Word	What the Noun Means	What the Verb Means
picture		
record		

1. Which artform is three-dimensional? Fill in the correct circle.

   (a) mural

   (b) cave painting

   (c) sculpture

   (d) none of these

2. Complete the analogy:

   _____ is

   to   **sculpture** _____

   as   **the Sistine Chapel** _____

   is to _____ .

3. Which of the "paintings" below is most like an example of abstract art? Fill in the correct circle.

   (a)

   (b)

   (c)

4. Prehistoric cave paintings never had words, only pictures. Look at the "cave painting" below. What do you think it is telling or showing? Write your answer on the lines below.

   _____

   _____

   _____

YOUR WORLD

It may be hard to imagine, but people existed long before words and written language did. Cave paintings were a way that prehistoric people recorded what they saw and did in the world around them before there was written language.

- Pretend that language were somehow wiped off the face of the Earth.
- Choose an event or activity in your life to make a record of.
- Make a "cave painting" of it.

Reading a Map

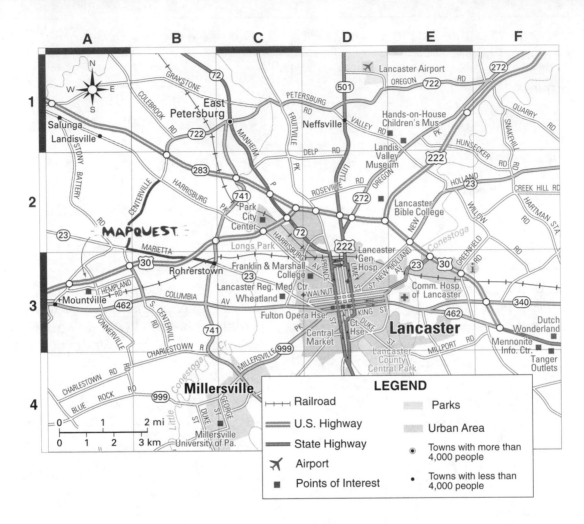

DIRECTION Maps usually have a **compass rose** that shows you which way is north. On most maps, like this one, it's straight up. The compass rose on this map is in the upper left corner.

DISTANCE Of course the distances on a map are much shorter than the distances in the real world. The **scale** shows you how to estimate the real distance. This map's scale is in the lower left corner.

PICTURES Maps usually have little pictures or symbols to represent real things like roads, towns, airports, or other points of interest. The map **legend** (or key) tells what they mean.

FINDING PLACES Rather than use latitude and longitude to locate features, many maps, like this one, use a **grid system** with numbers on one side and letters on another. An **index**, listing place names in alphabetical order, gives a letter and a number for each. The letter and number tell you which square to look for a place on the map's **grid**. For example, Landisville can be found at A-1 on this map.

USING THE MAP People use maps to help them travel from one place to another. What if you lived in East Petersburg and wanted to go to the Hands-on-House Children's Museum? First, locate the two places on the map. East Petersburg is in C-1, and Hands-on-House is in E-1. Next, look at the roads that connect them and decide on the best route. (There could be several different ways to go.) One possibility is to take Route 722 northeast to Petersburg Road. Take that east to Valley Road. And, finally, travel southeast on Valley Road until you get to the museum.

Find the following on page 92:

1. a type of flower	2. a direction
3. a city	4. a word in all capital letters
5. a word in **boldface**	6. a number spelled out
7. a street	8. a shape

Use words from page 92 to finish the following sentences:

9. A _____ tells you which direction on a map is north.

10. A _____ tells you how to know what the various symbols on a map represent.

11. If you want to know the distance that one inch of a map represents in area the map documents, look at the _____.

Name each of these things that you can find on many maps.

12. paved surfaces for cars	13. thousands of people living in the same general area
14. where you leave from if you're going to fly	15. has grass, might have a lake, open to the public

Find three words on page 92 related to each map part.

Compass Rose	Legend	Scale	Grid

Find the following on page 92:

1. an antonym for "higher"	2. a noun meaning "a part of the alphabet"
3. a compound word related to traveling	4. an adjective meaning "existing"
5. a suffix meaning "more than"	6. a synonym for "many"
7. a verb meaning "find"	8. an adverbial phrase meaning "instead of"

TAKE A CLOSER LOOK

Even if you'd never seen a map before, you would still have heard some of the terms, because many of them have other meanings. "Key," for example, can mean not only the part of a map that tells you what its symbols mean, but also the thing you use to open a locked door. When two or more words are spelled the same way and sound exactly the same, these words are called "homonyms." The map terms below have homonyms. Fill in the missing information.

Map Term	Meaning in the World of Maps	Other Meaning(s)
scale	tells you what the distances on a map are in the real world	
		1. a myth; 2. a very famous person

1. Which direction is indicated on the compass rose to the right?
   Fill in the correct circle.

   (a) south   (b) west   (c) southwest

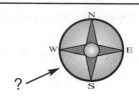

?

Use this map to answer questions 2–4. Fill in the correct circle to answer each question.

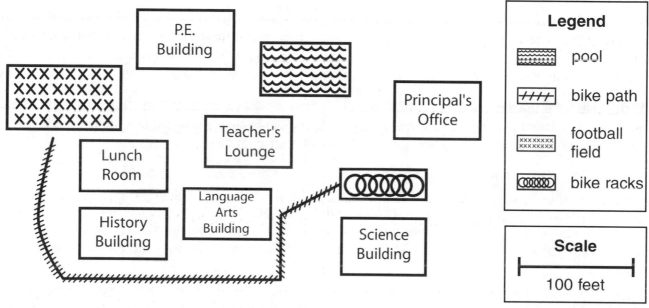

Legend

pool

bike path

football field

bike racks

Scale

100 feet

2. Which building is closest to the swimming pool?

   (a) the P.E. building

   (b) the History building

   (c) the Science building

3. About how far is it between the lunchroom and the principal's office?

   (a) 200 yards

   (b) 100 feet

   (c) 200 feet

4. Which part of campus can you take the bike path to (aside from the bike rack)?

   (a) the lunchroom

   (b) the football field

   (c) the pool

YOUR WORLD

A map can be made of absolutely any place—on land, under water, even in space. To make a good map, you need to keep only two things in mind: 1) make sure the information on the map is correct (for example, you don't want to put a mountain in a city that doesn't have any mountains); 2) make sure there is a way for someone looking at your map to translate the distances, symbols, etc., into real-world things.

• Make a map of a very small area with which you are very familiar. This can be anything from your neighborhood right down to your room.

• Be sure to include a compass rose, a scale, and a key.

Body Basics

Your body is made up of many different parts that work together every minute of every day and night. It's more amazing than any machine or computer. Even though everyone's body looks different outside, people have the same parts inside. Each system of the body has its own job. Some of the systems also work together to keep you healthy and strong.

CIRCULATORY SYSTEM In the circulatory system, the **heart** pumps **blood**, which then travels through tubes, called **arteries**, to all parts of the body. The blood carries the oxygen and food that the body needs to stay alive. **Veins** carry the blood back to the heart.

DIGESTIVE SYSTEM The digestive system moves food through parts of the body called the **esophagus**, **stomach**, and **intestines**. As the food passes through, some of it is broken down into tiny particles called **nutrients**, which the body needs. Nutrients enter the bloodstream, which carries them to all parts of the body. The digestive system then changes the remaining food into waste that is eliminated from the body.

ENDOCRINE SYSTEM The endocrine system includes glands that are needed for some body functions. There are two kinds of **glands**. Exocrine glands produce liquids such as sweat and saliva. **Endocrine** glands produce chemicals called hormones. **Hormones** control body functions, such as growth.

NERVOUS SYSTEM The nervous system enables us to think, feel, move, hear, and see. It includes the **brain**, the **spinal cord**, and **nerves** in all parts of the body. Nerves in the spinal cord carry signals back and forth between the brain and the rest of the body. The brain tells us what to do and how to respond. It has three major parts. The **cerebrum** controls thinking, speech, and vision. The **cerebellum** is responsible for physical coordination. The **brain stem** controls the respiratory, circulatory, and digestive systems.

RESPIRATORY SYSTEM The respiratory system allows us to breathe. Air comes into the body through the nose and mouth. It goes through the **windpipe** (or **trachea**) to two tubes (called **bronchi**), which carry air to the **lungs**. Oxygen from the air is taken in by tiny blood vessels in the lungs. The blood then carries oxygen to the cells of the body.

MUSCULAR SYSTEM Muscles are made up of elastic fibers There are three types of muscle: **skeletal**, **smooth**, and **cardiac**. The skeletal muscles help the body move—they are the large muscles we can see. Smooth muscles are found in our digestive system, blood vessels, and air passages. Cardiac muscle is found only in your heart. Smooth and cardiac muscles are involuntary muscles—they do their job without us having to think about them.

REPRODUCTIVE SYSTEM Through the reproductive system, adult human beings are able to create new human beings. Reproduction begins when a **sperm** cell from a man fertilizes an **egg** cell from a woman.

URINARY SYSTEM This system, which includes the **kidneys**, cleans waste from the blood and regulates the amount of water in the body.

IMMUNE SYSTEM The immune system protects your body from diseases by fighting against certain substances that come from outside, or **antigens**. This happens in different ways. For example, white blood cells called **B lymphocytes** learn to fight certain viruses and bacteria by producing **antibodies**, which spread around the body to attack them. Sometimes, as in **allergies**, the immune system makes a mistake and creates antibodies to fight a substance that's really harmless.

Find the following on page 96:

1. what you breathe	2. a child becomes an . . .
3. something you do with one of your five senses	4. what you're supposed to do in school
5. what you can do to earn money	6. a type of muscle
7. a prime number	8. something you find in the dairy aisle of a supermarket

Use words from page 96 to finish the following sentences:

9. Your blood travels through your _____ system in veins and
_____.

10. Your _____ clean waste from your blood.

11. Your _____ system fights viruses and bacteria by producing _____.

Name the body system that is best described by each of the following titles.

12. "My Heart Is Not on My Sleeve"	13. "The Bodybuilder's Best Friend"
14. "Whenever I Breathe Out"	15. "Sweating to the Oldies"

Find three words related to each body system.

Circulatory	Nervous	Immune	Digestive

Find the following on page 96:

1. an antonym for "front"	2. a noun that rhymes with "dude"
3. a verb meaning "says"	4. a homonym for where a prisoner is kept
5. a word having to do with perspiration that can be both a noun and a verb	6. a noun that is an anagram for "hams cot"
7. a drinkable noun	8. an adjective meaning "very bendable" or "flexible"

TAKE A CLOSER LOOK

You don't need to be a doctor to know something about what many things in the body do—all you need to do is know their names! For example, from the name "reproductive system," you know that something is reproduced—which, in this case, is us! Look at the "body words" below, list the word parts that you can separate out, then write what you can tell about the words based on what you know about their parts.

Body Words	Parts	What You Know from the Parts
circulatory system		
antibodies		

1. Which is not part of your digestive system? Fill in the correct circle.

  a

b

c

2. Complete the following analogy:

Your _____

is to your __circulatory system__

as your ____lungs____ are

to your _____.

3. Decode the pictograms below to reveal a famous saying by Rene Descartes. He believed that when we reflect on our own thoughts we can tell we exist apart from our bodies. Write your answer on the lines below.

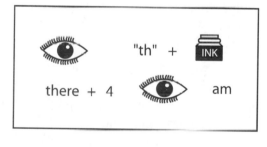

_____

_____

4. Blood circulates through your body. This means that it follows along a path and comes back to where it "started," only to keep moving along that same path again. The three main components of the circulatory system are **arteries, veins,** and the **heart.** Fill in the correct arrows to show the direction in which blood has to flow.

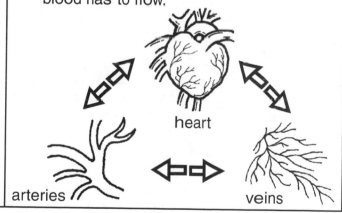

YOUR WORLD

What is the difference between people and machines? Are there things that are alike? Do they have systems for their "bodies" that resemble the systems in our bodies? Think about a car. What is its gasoline comparable to in our bodies? What about its oil?

- Imagine that you are a robot designer, and draw up a basic blueprint of a robot.
- How does it get power? How do its parts move? How does it know what to do? Base its "body systems" on our own.

Types of Music and Dance

Music

▶ **POP** Pop music (short for popular music) puts more emphasis on melody (tune) than does rock and has a softer beat. **Famous pop singers:** Frank Sinatra, Barbra Streisand, Madonna, Michael Jackson, Mariah Carey, Brandy, 'N Sync, Beyoncé Knowles, Jennifer Lopez, Britney Spears, Jessica Simpson.

▶ **RAP and HIP-HOP** In rap, words are spoken or chanted to a fast, hip-hop beat, with the emphasis on rhythm rather than melody. Rap was created in inner cities. The lyrics show strong feelings and may be about anger and violence. Hip-hop often includes "samples," which are pieces of music from other songs. **Famous rappers:** Eminem, Coolio, LL Cool J, TLC, The Fugees, Will Smith, Nelly, Jay-Z, Nas.

▶ **JAZZ** Jazz has its roots in the work songs, spirituals, and folk music of African-Americans. It began in the South in the early 1900s. **Famous jazz artists:** Louis Armstrong, Fats Waller, Jelly Roll Morton, Duke Ellington, Benny Goodman, Billie Holiday, Sarah Vaughan, Ella Fitzgerald, Dizzy Gillespie, Charlie Parker, Miles Davis, John Coltrane, Thelonious Monk, Wynton Marsalis.

▶ **ROCK** (also known as Rock 'n' Roll) Rock music, which started in the 1950s, is based on black rhythm and blues and country music. It often uses electronic instruments and equipment. Folk rock, punk, heavy metal, and alternative music are types of rock music. **Famous rock musicians:** Elvis Presley, Bob Dylan, Chuck Berry, The Beatles, Janis Joplin, The Rolling Stones, Joni Mitchell, Bruce Springsteen, Pearl Jam, Matchbox 20.

▶ **BLUES** The music called "the blues" developed from work songs and religious folk songs (spirituals) sung by African-Americans. It was introduced early in the 1900s by African-American musicians. Blues songs are usually sad. (A type of jazz is also called "the blues.") **Famous blues performers:** Ma Rainey, Bessie Smith, Billie Holiday, B. B. King, Muddy Waters, Robert Johnson, Howling Wolf, Etta James.

▶ **COUNTRY** American country music is based on Southern mountain music. Blues, jazz, and other musical styles have also influenced it. Country music became popular through the Grand Ole Opry radio show in Nashville, Tennessee, during the 1920s. **Famous country artists:** Hank Williams, Willie Nelson, Vince Gill, Reba McEntire, Tim McGraw, Faith Hill, Lee Ann Womack, Billy Gilman, Alan Jackson, Shania Twain, Dixie Chicks.

Dance

▶ **BALLET** Ballet is a kind of dance based on formal steps. The movements are often graceful and flowing. Ballets are almost always danced to music, are performed for an audience, and often tell a story. In the 15th century, ballet was part of the elaborate entertainment performed for the rulers of Europe. In the 1700s dancers wore bulky costumes and shoes with high heels. Women danced in hoopskirts—and so did men! In the 1800s ballet steps and costumes began to look the way they do now. Many of the most popular ballets today date back to the middle or late 1800s.

▶ **BALLROOM DANCING** Social dancing has been around since at least the Middle Ages, when it was popular at fairs and festivals. In the 1400s social dance was part of fancy court pageants. It developed into ballroom dances like the minuet and the waltz during the 1700s. More recent dances include the Charleston, lindy, twist, and tango, as well as disco dancing, break dancing, line dancing, and dances such as the macarena and electric slide.

▶ **MODERN DANCE** Modern dance differs from classical ballet. It is often less concerned with graceful, flowing movement and with stories. Modern dance steps are often not performed in traditional ballet. Dancers may put their bodies into awkward, angular positions and turn their backs on the audience. Many modern dances are based on ancient art, such as Greek sculpture, or on dance styles found in Africa and Asia.

▶ **FOLK DANCE** Folk dance is the term for a dance that is passed on from generation to generation and is part of the culture or way of life of people from a particular country or ethnic group. Virginia reel (American), czardas (Hungarian), jig, and the Israeli hora are some folk dances.

▶ **HIP HOP DANCE** Like the music, the driving rhythms and athletic moves of hip hop dance grew out of urban culture in New York City in the 1970s—break dancing and robot-like "popping and locking," are part of this tradition.

Find the following on page 100:

1. a time period	2. a state
3. a color	4. a number divisible by 2
5. a continent	6. a type of shoe
7. an animal (except beginning with a capital letter)	8. something you can climb

Use words from page 100 to finish the following sentences:

9. Spirituals and works songs were eventually developed into the type of music known as _____.

10. Popping and locking are part of the tradition of _____ dancing, which came out of the city of _____.

11. John Coltrane plays _____ music, which originated in the _____ in the early 1900s.

Name the type of music or dance based on the clue given.

12. a plural of a color	13. looks the same backwards or forwards
14. the Grand Ole Opry is part of the history	15. has been around for at least 600 years

Find three words on page 100 related to each form of music or dance. (Note: you may not use people.)

Rap	Ballet	Rock	Folk Dancing

Find the following on page 100:

1. an antonym for "outer"	2. a six-letter word whose only vowel is "Y"
3. an adjective meaning "very well-known"	4. a person's name that is an alliteration
5. a hyphenated phrase meaning "stiff and artificial-seeming"	6. a noun meaning "a group of observers"
7. a compound word in which each part is the same number of letters	8. a three-word proper noun that includes a type of food

TAKE A CLOSER LOOK

We know different types of music by certain names, but in all cases the style of music came first, and it was named only afterwards. For example, when Mozart was alive, he didn't think of himself as writing "classical" music—that's simply what music in that style and from that general time period was called later on. Look at the music terms below, all of which existed as words long before they were associated with a style of music. Write the definition of the word, then write out why you think this word was chosen to name the particular style of music it does today.

Music Term	"Non-musical" Meaning	Why This Term Goes with the Music
rap		
blues		

1. Solve these riddles to name two rock bands:

The Tumbling Boulders

Oyster-jewelry Jelly

2. Decode the pictograph below to name a musician/performer, then list what type of dance or music he or she is associated with.

Name:_____

Type:_____

3. Based on the information given on page 100, put the types of music and dance in chronological order, beginning with the oldest.

Types of Music/Dance	Chronological Order
jazz	
rock 'n' roll	
blues	
country	
ballet	
ballroom dancing	
hip-hop dancing	

4. Below is a map of the United States. There is enough information given on page 100 to name four types of music or dance that began in the U.S. Write at least three of them inside the map.

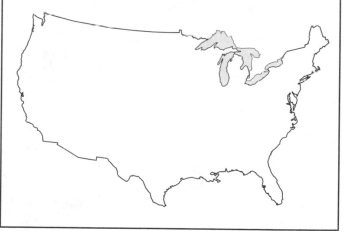

YOUR WORLD

People sing and dance for all sorts of reason, including to entertain, to celebrate, to mourn, and to tell a story. When have you danced and sung? Why? Write a paragraph on one of the following topics:

- the kind of dancing or singing you like to do best, and why
- the piece of music or dance that means the most to you, and why it does

Exercise

The CDC reports that the average kid spends 4.5 hours a day in front of some sort of screen (TV, video game, computer). That's 31.5 hours a week. In a year, that time adds up to 1,642.5 hours or 68.4 days! Can you find at least 30 minutes in your day to get some moderate exercise?

If you watch TV in the afternoons after school or on Saturday mornings, you've probably seen the "VERB. It's What You Do" ads. They're part of a seven-year campaign sponsored by the government to encourage kids age 9-13 to get more exercise.

Why does the U.S. Department of Health and Human Services' Centers for Disease Control and Prevention (CDC) think exercise is important for kids? In 2002, the National Center for Health Statistics reported that an estimated 8.8 million U.S. kids age 6–19 were overweight. Being overweight increases a risk of developing high blood pressure, diabetes, and heart disease.

But daily exercise has other benefits too: it makes you feel good. Exercise also helps you think better, sleep better, and feel more relaxed. Regular exercise will make you stronger and help you improve at physical activities. Breathing deeply during exercise gets more oxygen into your lungs with each breath. Your heart pumps more oxygen-filled blood all through your body with each beat. Muscles and joints get stronger and more flexible as you use them.

Organized sports are a good way to get a lot of exercise, but not the only way. You can shoot hoops, jog, ride a bike, or skate without being on a team. If you can't think of anything else, try walking in a safe place. Walk with friends or even try to get the adults in your life to put down the remote and join you. They could probably use the exercise!

Below are some activities, with a rough idea of how many calories a 100-pound person would burn per minute while doing them.

ACTIVITY	CALORIES PER MINUTE
Jogging (6 miles per hour)	8
Jumping rope (easy)	7
Playing basketball	7
Playing soccer	6
Bicycling (9.4 miles per hour)	5
Skiing (downhill)	5
Raking the lawn	4
Rollerblading (easy)	4
Walking (4 miles per hour)	4
Bicycling (5.5 miles per hour)	3
Swimming (25 yards per minute)	3
Walking (3 miles per hour)	3

Find the following on page 104:

1. a two-digit numeral	2. a word that starts and ends with "E"
3. a day of the week	4. a phrase in quotation marks
5. part of your body	6. something with wheels
7. a department of the U.S. government	8. 17.1 x 4 =

Use words from page 104 to finish the following sentences:

9. On average, kids spend _____ hours per day in front of one type of _____ or another.

10. The more you use _____ and _____, the stronger and more flexible they become.

11. More oxygen gets into your _____ when you exercise because you breathe _____ during it.

Guess the activity/exercise based on each statement. Only use activities listed on page 104.

12. You'll have a clean front yard.	13. You can score points by twos.
14. A motorboat is faster, but less of a workout.	15. It's just as healthy when it's called "football."

Find three words on page 104 related to each exercise-related concept.

Health	Movement	Body	Overweight

Find the following on page 104:

1. an adjective meaning "bendable"	2. an adverb meaning "every day"
3. a verb that can also be a noun that is something you wear on your wrist	4. a compound word meaning "too heavy"
5. initials that make a palindrome	6. a six-letter contraction
7. a word root meaning "circle" or "around"	8. a homonym for an antonym for "subtracts"

TAKE A CLOSER LOOK

You may not have heard of the present progressive, but you use it all the time. Every time you talk about an activity that has "-ing" at the end, you're using the present progressive. So, the present progressive is like exercise, in that it's active. (Sitting is the present progressive, too—but you get the idea!) With this in mind, take the seemingly passive nouns below and make them active with the present progressive. Then, describe the present progressive activity.

Noun	Present Progressive Activity	Description of Activity
bicycle		
ski		

1. Baseball can be good exercise, but you need special equipment to play it. However, there are two baseball terms that are types of exercise that you can do without any equipment at all (except maybe a pair of shoes). What are they?

_____   _____

2. Decode the pictograms to reveal a sentence about activity.

3. On page 104, there is a chart listing various activities and how many calories per minute they burn (for an average 100-pound person). Some of that information has been used for the bar graph below, each bar representing an activity. Write the name of the activity inside each bar. One of the answers has been provided for you.

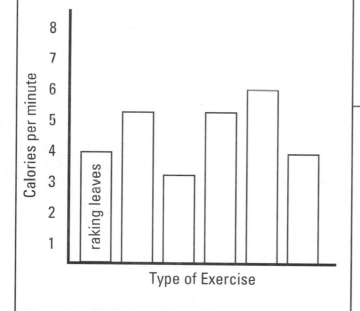

4. In 2002, the National Center for Health Statistics estimated that 8.8 million American kids ages 6–19 were overweight. If an equal amount of kids of each age within that age range are overweight, how many overweight 12-year-olds are there in the U.S.? (Round to the nearest thousand.)

_____

YOUR WORLD

Everybody in the world has to sleep and eat. You also go to school. All of these things take time. What else takes up your time? How much time do you spend each week exercising?

- Guess how many hours per week you exercise, and write your guess down. Don't just pick a number at random, but sit down and try to figure it out.

- Keep a journal for a week of everything you do that is exercise (which includes walking), and see how this compares to your original guess—and, more importantly, if it's at least 30 minutes a day.

Answer Key

DNA

Page 9
1. 1953, 2000
2. X, Y
3. scientist, researchers
4. 3.1 billion
5. eyes, hair, DNA, etc.
6. parents, children, identical twins
7. 46
8. a roundworm
9. X
10. molecules
11. chromosomes; parents
12. Francis Crick
13. James Watson
14. XY
15. 30,000–40,000

Page 10
Genes: code, rod-like, molecules, etc.
Chromosomes: genes, pairs, male, etc.
Scientists: Francis Crick, discovered, James Watson, etc.
Cells: DNA, molecule, structure, etc.
1. organism
2. Francis Crick, James Watson, U.S. Human Genome Project, etc.
3. pairs, twins
4. identical
5. U.S.
6. tall, short
7. rod-like
8. species

Page 11
1. b. 1,000
2. human genome
3. $(46 - (22 \times 2)) + 0 = 2$
4. Accept reasonable answers. Answer given on page 8 include color of eyes, color of hair, height, and chance of getting certain diseases.

What's Out There

Page 13
1. black
2. hundreds of light years, 600 miles
3. 50 billion, 200 billion
4. 76 years
5. Earth, Mars, Jupiter
6. asteroids
7. 2061
8. planetary, emission, dark, reflection
9. meteoroid; meteorite
10. satellite; orbits
11. gravity
12. the Asteroid Belt
13. a black hole
14. a comet
15. gravity

Page 14
Nebulas: fuzzy, emission, cluster, etc.
Comets: ice, dust, rock, etc.
Black Holes: gravity, X-ray, supermassive, etc.
Galaxies: stars, gas, billion, etc.
1. boulder
2. super-
3. blew
4. artificial
5. interstellar
6. creating
7. collapse
8. completely

Page 15
1. the sun; a galaxy
2. satellites
3. galaxies; gas; asteroids; comets; clouds; stars; space
4. Accept reasonable answers.

Biodiversity

Page 17
1. 4,000, 9,000, 5,200, etc.
2. biodiversity, life, variety, etc.
3. species
4. 0.6 inches, 12 inches
5. Earth, Venus
6. 2003
7. the Pacific
8. 242
9. life
10. Homo sapiens
11. beetles
12. turtle (tortise)
13. ape
14. seahorse
15. ostrich

Page 18
Birds: perching, raptors, penguins, etc.
Plants: flowering, evergreens, species, etc.
Mammals: rodents, bats, monkeys, etc.
Arthropods: insects, spiders, butterflies, etc.
1. all
2. variety
3. everywhere, flytrap, evergreens, etc.
4. orang
5. just
6. estimates
7. bats
8. southeastern

Page 19
1. a
2. Venus flytrap
3. d
4. a penguin

Animal Migration

Page 21
1. 90, 46
2. migration, hummingbird, cranes, etc.
3. Antarctica, the Arctic, Alaska
4. 2,500
5. 46 mph, 1 mph
6. 22,000-mile
7. great-great-grandchildren
8. swallows
9. animals
10. south; 90 days
11. saltwater
12. long-tailed jaeger
13. arctic tern
14. humpback whale
15. bird

Page 22
Bird: fly, diving, search, etc.
Fish: spawn, saltwater, smell, etc.
Whale: humpback, socialize, subtropical, etc.
Insect: butterflies, flying, warm, etc.
1. they
2. and
3. tern
4. mon-
5. mph
6. around
7. following
8. Hawaii

Page 23
1. humpback whale
2. eels; anadromous
3. hummingbird, crane, swallow, arctic tern
4. Accept reasonable answers.

Clouds

Page 25
1. December
2. blue, gray, mackerel, etc.
3. *cirrus*, *stratus*, etc.
4. Luke Howard
5. 20,000 ft., 6,500 ft., etc.
6. hair
7. nephology
8. contrails
9. fish scales
10. Luke Howard
11. water; ice
12. cumulus
13. cirrus
14. altostratus
15. nimbostratus

Page 26
Latin: *cirrus, cumulus, stratus,* etc.
Water: ice, moisture, droplets, etc.
Contrails: condensation, man-made, exhaust, etc.
1. -logy
2. man-made
3. puffy
4. period
5. generally
6. altocumulus
7. biggest
8. darker, distinguishing

Page 27
1. Who is Luke Howard?
2. nephology
3. Accept reasonable answers.
4. upper left oval: cirro/-us; bottom oval: alto

Sources of Energy

Answer Key

Page 29
1. Earth
2. 85%
3. Pennsylvania
4. 700 degrees
5. 700
6. researcher
7. Saudi Arabia
8. 2002
9. sunlight
10. nuclear, Chernobyl
11. wood, switchgrass
12. nuclear energy
13. fossil fuels
14. biomass energy
15. geothermal energy

Page 30
Fossil Fuels: oil, coal, gas, pumpjack, etc.
Nuclear: fission, atoms, reactor, accident, etc.
Water: rivers, streams, dams, turbine, etc.
Biomass: wood, straw, ethanol, etc.
Geothermal: volcanoes, hot springs, mantle, etc.
Wind: windmills, blades, generators, etc.
Solar: sunlight, silicon, cells, etc.
1. geyser
2. import
3. ology
4. mantle
5. drawback
6. alfalfa
7. gradually
8. active

Page 31
1. b
2. a
3. Accept reasonable responses. Sample answers include: petroleum, mantle, Earth, hydroelectric, cells, switchgrass, solar, reactor.
4. Reasons include: takes up little ground space, doesn't pollute, doesn't get used up, etc. shortcoming—not always windy

Governments Around the World

Page 33
1. democracy, monarchy, etc.
2. the United Kingdom, Saudi Arabia, Cuba, etc.
3. one
4. all-powerful
5. U.S.
6. demos, kratia
7. throne
8. Winston Churchill
9. monarchy; queen
10. dictator; Germany
11. population; Communist
12. democracy
13. monarchy
14. Communist
15. democracy/constitutional monarchy

Page 34
Democracy: people, representative, parliament, etc.

Monarchy: king, hereditary, ceremonial, etc.
Totalitarian: all-powerful, dictator, little freedom, etc.
Communist: totalitarian, Communist party, control, etc.
1. family
2. pick
3. some
4. Mexico
5. mon-
6. everyday
7. cabinet
8. when

Page 35
1. b
2. monarchy; dictator
3. Winston Churchill
4. United States, Canada, United Kingdom, Japan

The Middle East

Page 37
1. Spain, France, Israel, etc.
2. 1945
3. Egyptians, Jews, Muslims, etc.
4. Alexander the Great, King David, etc.
5. WWI or II, Arab-Israeli Wars, etc.
6. Islam
7. cuneiform, hieroglyphics
8. the Code of Hammurabi
9. Muhammad; 632
10. 1948; attacked (invaded)
11. the Sumerian peoples; Iraq
12. Moses
13. the Romans
14. Alexander the Great
15. Charles Martel

Page 38
Ottoman Turks: Muslims, empire, huge, etc.
Muslims: Arabia, Muhammad, Mecca, etc.
Egyptians: pyramids, hieroglyphics, pharaohs, etc.
Jews: Israel, Palestine, Holocaust, etc.
1. huge
2. begins
3. writing
4. gradually
5. under
6. world's
7. invade
8. spreads

Page 39
1. King David, Alexander the Great
2. d
3. B, C, E, F, D, A
4. The Ottoman Empire

Native Americans

Page 41
1. Oklahoma, Alaska, etc.
2. 1830, 1910, etc.
3. 16,000
4. today
5. Columbus
6. 850,000
7. bridge
8. hunger

9. 20,000
10. Mississippi
11. Indians; the East Indies
12. North Carolina
13. Alabama
14. Tennessee
15. Georgia

Page 42
Europeans: diseases, wars, explorers, etc.
"Trail of Tears": Cherokee, hunger, etc.
U.S. Government: Indian Removal Act, citizenship, Congress, etc.
"Indians": explorers, East Indies, Asia, etc.
1. hot
2. soldiers
3. sea
4. many
5. homelands
6. quarter
7. increased
8. dramatically

Page 43
1. c. 2000
2. c. 630,000
3. Trail of Tears
4. b. 4,000

U.S. Constitution

Page 45
1. 1787, 1789
2. 10
3. www.house.gov/Constitution/ Constitution.html
4. president
5. office
6. legislative, judicial, executive (any one)
7. courts
8. American
9. Preamble
10. amendments; the Bill of Rights
11. Article 5
12. 2
13. 6 or 7
14. 4
15. 3

Page 46
Article 1: Senate, House of Representatives, legislative, etc.
Article 2: executive, president, Electoral College, etc.
Article 3: Supreme Court, powers, Judicial, etc.
Article 6: federal, supreme, state, etc.
1. short
2. liberty
3. defense
4. we
5. establish
6. more
7. tranquility
8. judicial

Answer Key

Page 47
1. b (1789)
2. a. Congress
3. gun (2nd), soldier (3rd), newspaper (1st)
4. the First Amendment

Nobel Prizes
Page 49
1. 1833, 2002, etc.
2. Alfred B. Nobel
3. chemistry, literature, etc.
4. Swedish, Tibetan, etc.
5. the Russo-Japanese War
6. democracy
7. Jimmy Carter, F.W. de Klerk, etc.
8. Martin Luther King Jr.
9. Sweden, dynamite
10. 1993; Nelson Mandela
11. Doctors without Borders, UNICEF, UN, Int'l Campaign to Ban Landmines (any two)
12. Jimmy Carter
13. Woodrow Wilson
14. Theodore Roosevelt
15. F.W. de Klerk

Page 50
Dalai Lama: Buddhist, exile, Tibetan, etc.
Nelson Mandela: 1993, blacks, leader, etc.
Rigoberta Menchú Tum: rights, Guatemala, peasant, etc.
Shirin Ebadi: women, Islamic, rights, etc.
1. peace
2. for, to
3. Woodrow Wilson
4. first
5. her, she
6. they, who
7. ex-
8. Islamic

Page 51
1. B
2. a
3. b
4. Accept reasonable answers.

Getting to the Root
Page 53
1. English, Greek, Latin
2. stem, root(s)
3. biology, psychology, etc.
4. Earth
5. aquarium
6. television
7. microscope, telescope
8. prescription
9. root
10. prefix
11. Latin; full of
12. -mem-
13. -psych-
14. -phon-
15. -bio-

Page 54
Root: stem, meaning, basic, etc.
Prefix: beginning, Latin, parts, etc.
Suffix: end, Greek, word, etc.
1. see
2. pre-
3. without
4. complete
5. water
6. it
7. probably
8. photograph

Page 55
1. autograph
2. euphonic
3. microscope: micro = small, scope = see
4. telephone: tele = far away, phone = sound

Words About Words
Page 57
1. sandwich, melon, etc.
2. dog, person
3. Clint Eastwood, Daniel Handler
4. big, small
5. baker, author, etc.
6. letters
7. radar, radio
8. two
9. eponym
10. know
11. acronym
12. pseudonym
13. cliché
14. homophone
15. palindrome

Page 58
Euphemism: pleasant, in place of, Senior citizen, etc.
Cliché: saying, used so often, lack of interest, etc.
Acronym: abbreviation, letters, Radar, etc.
Anagram: word, rearranging, nonsense, etc.
1. different
2. phrase
3. pleasant
4. the Earl of Sandwich, *A Series of Unfortunate Events,* etc.
5. way
6. many
7. have
8. humorous

Page 59
1. c
2. Shaquille O'Neal
3. pseudonym
4. cliché: "If you can't say something…"; eponym: sandwich; homophones (pair): see/sea; acronym and palindrome: radar (which appears twice)

All About Books
Page 61
1. pages, letters, paper
2. Germany, China
3. store
4. emperor
5. hand
6. the Middle Ages, the 19th century, etc.
7. press, linotype
8. paper towels
9. scrolls
10. China
11. monks; parchment
12. 19th century
13. 100 A.D.
14. Middle Ages
15. 1450s

Page 62
Monks: illuminations, read, parchment, etc.
Printing: press, Germany, common, etc.
Codex: pages, stitched, easier, etc.
Typesetting: ink, press, hand, etc.
1. big
2. priests
3. search
4. expensive
5. especially
6. animal skins
7. buy
8. everyone

Page 63
1. c
2. scrolls, codex, press, ink, pages
3. paper; Middle Ages

Computer Talk
Page 65
1. web
2. cookie
3. magazine, newspapers, etc.
4. kilo
5. (tele)phone
6. bytes
7. spam
8. virus
9. encryption
10. disappears
11. pixel or picture element, smallest
12. read only memory
13. random access memory
14. personal digital assistant
15. Hyper Text Markup Language

Page 66
Internet: worldwide, networks, linked, etc.
Chip: silicon, information, circuits, etc.
Bookmark: browser, Website, typing, etc.
Cookie: information, Website, preferences, etc.
1. hard
2. k
3. download
4. smallest
5. wire
6. store
7. inter-
8. crypt

Answer Key

Page 67
1. b
2. portal
3. glitch, hacker, ROM, megabyte, encryption, error, browser, blog
4. kilobyte; 1,000 bytes of data

Calendar Basics
Page 69
1. 46 B.C.E., 2004, etc.
2. garnet, opal, etc.
3. rat, ox, etc.
4. XIII
5. Mars
6. 365, 622, etc.
7. aperire, septem, etc.
8. Julian calendar, Gregorian calendar
9. Islamic; Gregorian
10. Earth; the moon
11. Pope Gregory XIII; 1582
12. July
13. January
14. November
15. June

Page 70
Islamic: A.D. 622, Muharram, 1424, etc.
Chinese: Rat, Ox, Dragon, etc.
Julian: Julius Caesar, sun, revised, etc.
Gregorian: Pope Gregory XIII, leap year, world, etc.
1. 11	5. ox
2. leap	6. aqua-
3. ago	7. divided
4. special	8. equivalent

Page 71
1. 9 (novem)
2. beginning of the Jewish calendar; beginning of the Julian calendar; beginning of the Islamic calendar; Pope Gregory XII revises Julian calendar/beginning of the Gregorian calendar
3. Muharram
4. Rosh Hashanah; the Gregorian calendar

The Metric System
Page 73
1. 1/1000, 1/100, etc.
2. meter, liter, gram
3. 1795, 1960
4. 2.54, 30.48, etc.
5. square
6. liter
7. prefix
8. 10,000
9. standardized; 1795
10. shorter; kilometer
11. grams; two
12. millimeter
13. decimeter
14. centiliter
15. hectogram

Page 74
Length: meter, kilometer, etc.
Weight: mass, gram, etc.
Area: square meter, hecatres, etc.
Volume: liter, gram, etc.
1. deka-
2. kg
3. France, International System of Units
4. rough
5. most
6. basic
7. acres
8. cubic centimeter
dekayear; decade
hectoyear; century
kiloyear; millenium

Page 75
1. 10; 10,000
2. 7.6 cm
3. b. Eric (because he can run a longer distance in the same amount of time it takes Greggory to run a shorter distance)
4. Kevin Garnett; Moses Malone; Karl Malone

Money Around the World
Page 77
1. Austria, Belgium, etc.
2. Europe
3. "euro"
4. $1.22
5. spring
6. twelve
7. U.K.
8. pizza
9. European Union; euro
10. Canada; the U.S.
11. Exchange rates
12. peso
13. yen
14. euro
15. euro

Page 78
Euro: Austria, Belgium, Finland, etc.
Animals: tiger, elephant, cows, etc.
Coins: obverse, reverse, symbol, etc.
Exchange Rates: convert, exports, travel, etc.
1. EU	5. have
2. Austria	6. -est
3. Greece	7. expensive
4. they	8. on, in

Page 79
1. a
2. d
3. March; July
4. Great Britain, Denmark, Sweden

Primes, Percents, Fractions, & Fractals
Page 81
1. 10%, 24%
2. 1, 2, 3, 4
3. 1975
4. mathematician
5. coastlines, mountains
6. 72
7. French
8. 100, 25
9. prime; itself
10. Fractal geometry
11. reducing; lowest common denominator
12. fractal
13. numerator
14. 2
15. 4/5

Page 82
Primes: 1, itself, divided, etc.
Percents: per, hundred, divide, etc.
Fractions: numerator, denominator, reduce, etc.
Fractals: self-repeated, patterns, shapes, etc.
1. give
2. Benoit Mandelbrot
3. micro-
4. let's
5. only
6. structure
7. algebraic
8. infinite

Page 83
1. b
2. c 1/8
3. fractions, percents
4. Accept reasonable answers.

Finding the Area
Page 85
1. square, circle, etc.
2. equal, "The Greek letter [etc.]"
3. 2000 B.C.
4. ½
5. four
6. pi
7. 28.26
8. the Babylonians
9. base; height
10. quadrilateral; right angles
11. circumference; center
12. triangle
13. parallelogram or rectangle
14. square
15. circle

Page 86
Quadrilateral: square, rectangle, equal, etc.
Squared: side, right angle, formula, etc.Base: multiply, triangle, height, etc.
Pi: circle, Greek, diameter, etc.

Answer Key

1. tri-
2. not-so-secret
3. find
4. quad-
5. unlike
6. the
7. right
8. plane

"parallel" + gram (line); having parallel lines

"rect" (right) + angle; having right angles

Page 87
1. 100 square miles
2. a
3. Accept reasonable answers.
4. square; parallelogram

Through Artists' Eyes
Page 89
1. 1940, 1508, 1512
2. the Statue of Liberty
3. Lascaux, Rome
4. food
5. the Bible
6. funny
7. photos
8. humans
9. 17,000
10. nature; people
11. Michelangelo; fresco
12. photography
13. painting
14. sculpture
15. cave painting

Page 90
Painting: still life, abstract, portrait, etc.
Sculpture: three-dimensional, metal, clay, etc.
Fresco: plaster, Michelangelo, wall, etc.
Mural: walls, paint, brightening, etc.
1. world
2. pre-
3. small
4. don't
5. artists
6. too
7. masterpiece
8. tradition

Page 91
1. c
2. the Statue of Liberty; fresco
3. b
4. Accept reasonable answers.

Reading a Map
Page 93
1. rose
2. north, left, etc.
3. Landisville, East Petersburg
4. reading, direction, etc.
5. scale, legend, etc.
6. one, two
7. Petersburg Rd., Valley Rd.
8. square
9. compass rose
10. legend/key
11. scale
12. roads
13. town/city
14. airport
15. park

Page 94
Compass Rose: north, south, east, etc.
Legend: pictures, road, highway, etc.
Scale: distance, estimate, shorter, etc.
Grid: letters, numbers, system, etc.
1. lower
2. letter
3. airports
4. real
5. -er
6. several
7. locate
8. rather than

Page 95
1. c. southwest
2. a. the P.E. building
3. c. 200 feet
4. b. the football field

Body Basics
Page 97
1. air, oxygen
2. adult
3. see, feel, hear
4. learn
5. job
6. skeletal, smooth, or cardiac
7. two, three
8. egg
9. circulatory; arteries
10. kidneys
11. immune; antibodies
12. circulatory
13. muscular
14. respiratory
15. endocrine

Page 98
Circulatory: heart, blood, veins, etc.
Nervous: brain, nerves, signals, etc.
Immune: antibodies, protects, allergies, etc.
Digestive: food, stomach, nutrients, etc.
1. back
2. food
3. tells
4. cell
5. sweat
6. stomach
7. water
8. elastic

Page 99
1. b
2. heart; respiratory system
3. "I think, therefore I am."
4. Arrows should be filled in to show that blood flows from heart to arteries, from arteries to veins, and from veins to heart.

Music & Dance
Page 101
1. 15th century, 1700, 1970s, etc.
2. Virginia, Tennessee
3. black
4. 20
5. Europe, Africa, Asia
6. high heels
7. wolf
8. mountain
9. the blues
10. hip-hop; New York
11. jazz; South
12. blues
13. pop
14. country
15. ballroom dancing

Page 102
Rap: spoken, anger, rhythm, etc.
Ballet: graceful, story, costumes, etc.
Rock: electronic, punk, alternative, etc.
Folk Dancing: culture, ethnic, generation, etc.
1. inner
2. rhythm
3. famous
4. Janis Joplin
5. robot-like
6. audience
7. ballroom, ballet
8. Jelly Roll Morton

Page 103
1. The Rolling Stones and Pearl Jam
2. Eminem; rap/hip-hop
3. ballroom and ballet, blues and jazz, country, rock 'n' roll, hip-hop dancing
4. in the U.S.: jazz, blues, country, hip-hop dancing

Exercise
Page 105
1. 30, 13, etc.
2. exercise
3. Saturday
4. "VERB. It's what you do."
5. lungs, muscles, etc.
6. bike
7. U.S. Dept. of Health and Human Services
8. 68.4
9. 4.5; screen
10. muscles; joints
11. lungs; deeply
12. raking the lawn
13. basketball
14. swimming
15. soccer

Page 106
Health: stronger, flexible, relaxed, etc.
Movement: jog, skate, ride, etc.
Body: heart, muscles, joints, etc.
Overweight: diabetes, disease, high blood pressure, etc.
1. flexible
2. daily
3. watch
4. overweight
5. CDC
6. they're
7. cycle
8. ads

Page 107
1. run; walk
2. Football and basketball are great exercise.
3. [left to right:] rollerblading or raking the lawn, skiing, jogging, basketball, rollerblading or raking the lawn
4. 629,000